CW00469070

The Financial Times E:

Budgeting and Forecasting

PEARSON

At Pearson, we believe in learning – all kinds of learning for all kinds of people. Whether it's at home, in the classroom or in the workplace, learning is the key to improving our life chances.

That's why we're working with leading authors to bring you the latest thinking and the best practices, so you can get better at the things that are important to you. You can learn on the page or on the move, and with content that's always crafted to help you understand quickly and apply what you've learned.

If you want to upgrade your personal skills or accelerate your career, become a more effective leader or more powerful communicator, discover new opportunities or simply find more inspiration, we can help you make progress in your work and life.

Pearson is the world's leading learning company. Our portfolio includes the Financial Times, Penguin, Dorling Kindersley, and our educational business, Pearson International.

Every day our work helps learning flourish, and wherever learning flourishes, so do people.

To learn more please visit us at: **www.pearson.com/uk**

The Financial Times Essential Guide to Budgeting and Forecasting

How to deliver accurate numbers

Nigel Wyatt

PEARSON

Harlow, England • London • New York • Boston • San Francisco • Toronto • Sydney
Auckland • Singapore • Hong Kong • Tokyo • Seoul • Taipei • New Delhi
Cape Town • São Paulo • Mexico City • Madrid • Amsterdam • Munich • Paris • Milan

PEARSON EDUCATION LIMITED

Edinburgh Gate
Harlow CM20 2JE
Tel: +44 (0)1279 623623
Fax: +44 (0)1279 431059
Website: www.pearson.com/uk

First published in Great Britain in 2012

© Pearson Education Limited 2012

The right of Nigel Wyatt to be identified as author of this work has been asserted by him in accordance with the Copyright, Designs and Patents Act 1988.

Pearson Education is not responsible for the content of third-party internet sites.

ISBN: 978-0-273-76813-5

British Library Cataloguing-in-Publication Data
A catalogue record for this book is available from the British Library

Library of Congress Cataloging-in-Publication Data
Wyatt, Nigel.
 The financial times essential guide to budgeting and forecasting : how to deliver accurate numbers / Nigel Wyatt.
   p. cm.
 Includes bibliographical references and index.
 ISBN 978-0-273-76813-5 (pbk. : alk. paper) 1. Budget in business. 2. Business forecasting.
3. Business planning. I. Title.
 HG4028.B8W93 2012
 658.15'4--dc23

                          2012019642

All rights reserved. No part of this publication may be reproduced, stored in a retrieval system, or transmitted in any form or by any means, electronic, mechanical, photocopying, recording or otherwise, without either the prior written permission of the publisher or a licence permitting restricted copying in the United Kingdom issued by the Copyright Licensing Agency Ltd, Saffron House, 6–10 Kirby Street, London EC1N 8TS. This book may not be lent, resold, hired out or otherwise disposed of by way of trade in any form of binding or cover other than that in which it is published, without the prior consent of the publisher.

All trademarks used herein are the property of the respective owners. The use of any trademark in this text does not vest in the author or publisher any trademark ownership rights in such trademarks, nor does the use of such trademarks imply any affiliation with or endorsement of this book by such owners.

The Financial Times. With a worldwide network of highly respected journalists, *The Financial Times* provides global business news, insightful opinion and expert analysis of business, finance and politics. With over 500 journalists reporting from 50 countries worldwide, our in-depth coverage of international news is objectively reported and analysed from an independent, global perspective. To find out more, visit www.ft.com/pearsonoffer

10 9 8 7 6 5 4 3
16 15 14

Typeset in ITC Stone Serif Std 8.75/12pt by 3
Printed by Ashford Colour Press Ltd, Gosport

Contents

part 3 Reviewing your budgeting and forecasting performance

About the author

Nigel Wyatt is an accountant who has owned and run his own financial training consultancy, Magenta Financial Training since 1992: www.Magentanetwork.co.uk. He works with a wide range of organisations, including many blue-chip companies. In recent years he has worked extensively internationally, including training in India, China, Oman, Saudi Arabia, UAE, Thailand and Malaysia.

Praise for *The Financial Times Essential Guide to Budgeting and Forecasting*

'A concise and highly readable primer on budgetary control, based on years of experience in running training courses for non-financial managers.'

Terry Clark, *CFO, Trade Extensions*

'This is a timely book written by Nigel, we are living in a changing and more challenging global world, with ever more pressures on managers to perform and complete demanding budgets. This is a practical book that managers at all levels will benefit from and learn the pitfalls of budgeting and forecasting. This book also addresses the changing and evolving world with a good section on beyond budgeting – a new and little unknown concept beginning to gain momentum. A must read book.'

Manjit Biant, *management consultant*

'Love them or hate them, budgets are part of the corporate landscape. If you're working in a finance department or managing a profit centre in an organisation the chances are budgets are an inescapable part of your life. Despite some fierce criticism in recent years well designed budgetary control systems still have a place in the modern business. Nigel Wyatt's book makes a strong case that budgeting can still prove an invaluable tool for focusing strategic thinking and managing your business – and the book gives some great tips and advice on how to use them and get the best from them.'

Paul Lower FCMA FInstLM, *former FD and business coach*

'This book is an excellent tool for those responsible for preparing budgets and forecast within their organisations. It takes you through the process of budgeting and forecasting without the need of having an accounting knowledge or qualification. Its approach is from a practical point of view with very stimulating examples in order to assimilate the concepts and focus on your own organisation.'

Juan Carlos Venegas ICPA CFC ICFS IPFM, *accountant, forensic consultant, counter fraud specialist and fraud examiner*

Acknowledgements

We are grateful to the following for permission to reproduce copyright material:

Tables

Table 2.1 from Enterprise Performance Management Research Series, The Hackett Group, 2008–2011; Table 11.1 from 12 Beyond Budgeting Principles (2011), **http://www.bbrt.org/beyond-budgeting/bb-principles.html**.

The Financial Times

Article on page 44 from Kodak's inability to evolve led to its demise, *The Financial Times*, 20/01/2012 (Waters, R.).

In some instances we have been unable to trace the owners of copyright material, and we would appreciate any information that would enable us to do so.

Introduction

Is this book right for me?

This book will be useful for anyone with an involvement in budgets or forecasts. If you have just been given a budget for the first time, or you have had a budget for a number of years but have never received any formal training about what you should be doing, then this book is for you.

Perhaps you have already considerable budgeting experience, you may be an experienced finance professional but would like to review your practice against some of the latest ideas. You might like your views and ideas tested with an alternative explanation of good practice for budgeting and forecasting. If any of this is true, then this book is for you.

Maybe you support others who build or manage budgets, or who are involved in forecasting. This book will give you a valuable insight into their requirements so that you can support them better.

The book also includes useful information for people working with budgets at a senior or strategic level. There is content on effective delegation of budgets and designing systems and approaches to help managers deliver the most out of their budgets.

How do I know it will help me with my particular situation?

This book actively coaches you through all of the stages of building, managing and evaluating budgets and forecasts. Through the book you will be prompted with numerous questions that encourage you to think about your own situation and, more importantly, put the concepts and ideas into practice. This book is designed to enable you to make a difference and an improvement within your organisation.

It will cover your impact on costs, income, profit (known as surplus in not-for-profit organisations) and cash.

The book is divided into three parts:

- Part 1: Preparing your budgets
- Part 2: Managing your budget and delivering performance
- Part 3: Reviewing your budgeting and forecasting performance.

In the first instance we recommend you work through the book in sequence, rather than picking out sections. After you have done that it can be used as a quick, handy, reference guide when required.

Part 1: Preparing your budgets

This part lays out the vital background to budgeting and forecasts. It gives you the knowledge and skills to build effective budgets and forecasts. You will also be coached on how to evaluate and improve your personal performance. The production, evaluation and improvement of forecasting are areas of weakness within many organisations so Chapter 2 is dedicated to addressing this in detail.

Part 2: Managing your budget and delivering performance

In this part of the book we focus on the practical aspects of controlling and managing a budget, including steps you can take to try to make savings with the lowest impact on your service or organisation.

This part focuses on the day-to-day management of your budgets, and how you can become more practised at addressing issues before they become a crisis.

Part 3: Reviewing your budgeting and forecasting performance

This book is about making improvements in your budgeting and forecasting to have a real impact on you and your organisation. In the final part of the book we challenge you to review your learning and continue the coaching approach to encourage you to deliver some measureable improvements in your budgeting and forecasting.

Take responsibility for your own training and personal development and start learning from this book today.

part

Preparing your budgets

Cap Ex
Training
External support
Pay rises
Bonuses

1

What is the budget for?

The budget is the bane of corporate America. It never should have existed.

But the budgeting process at most companies has to be the most ineffective practice in management. It sucks the energy, time, fun and big dreams out of an organisation. ... And yet ... companies sink countless hours into writing budgets. What a waste.

Jack Welch, former CEO General Electric

Why do we need budgets? What is their role? Budgets can have many functions so first you must determine what the role of your budget is within your organisation. Then you can decide what the correct approach to building the budget or managing it should be.

Introduction

There is a popular view amongst many managers and even finance directors that budgets do not work well and may be harmful. There is even an approach called 'beyond budgeting' which advocates the scrapping of budgets completely. (There is more about the ideas behind 'beyond budgeting' in Chapter 11.)

Despite the problems with budgets, most companies and finance directors could not imagine a world without them. In this book we seek to make the budgeting process less painful and more productive for you and your organisation. We will coach you, asking you, with the help of short exercises and questions, to consider your own situation and organisation, and more importantly identify approaches and solutions that are right for you.

You can also use many of the exercises with your team members to encourage them to seek improvements in the budgeting and forecasting process. This book covers forecasting in Chapter 2 where we focus on how to make it effective and discuss how it relates to the budgeting process. We will give you the tools to build budgets (Chapter 4) and manage budgets (Chapter 7). But first of all, the starting point has to be to define exactly what the budget is for.

The role of budgets – why do we have them?

If we were to ask people what the word 'budget' means we would get a range of answers. The word has a number of meanings: to the lay person it could mean cheap (often associated with inferior quality) or cost saving. The vocabulary of budgeting might distort and colour our views about how we should go about building and managing budgets. Therefore, before deciding how we go about building or managing a budget, it is important to understand exactly what the budget is trying to achieve; in other words 'What are the objectives of the budget?'

There are many roles that a budget may perform and it may have subtly different roles in different organisations.

Exercise

Take a blank sheet of paper and spend a few minutes listing out what you think the roles of the budget are within your organisation. Then try to rank these in order of importance. Review your answer against our list below.

We often find many managers identify the primary role of the budget as being to control costs. Having this view gives us a particular attitude as to how we build and manage budgets. In fact there are many roles the budget could perform, including the following:

1 Meeting the organisation's objectives
2 Planning
3 Monitoring and controlling
4 Co-ordinating

5 Evaluating performance

6 Improving performance

7 Motivating managers

8 A management contract

9 Communicating

10 Providing a basis for authorising expenditure and delegating responsibility

11 Identifying scarce resources

12 Allocating resources

13 Demonstrating and delivering good corporate governance.

The fact that a budget may be performing so many potential roles is why budgets often fail in some respect. There may be a good case for having different figures for different purposes. This could be very confusing, but an organisation may have additional targets beyond the budget. Some typical examples could be:

■ stretched sales targets for salespeople that exceed the budget

■ key performance indicators (KPIs)

■ unit cost targets

■ cost reduction targets.

An organisation might also make extensive use of forecasts (forecasts and budgets are different: for further details see Chapter 2).

Each of a budget's potential roles can be reviewed as follows.

1 Meeting the organisation's objectives

The principal reason why an organisation chooses to have a budgetary control system is to enable it to achieve its objectives. Therefore, a starting point for any budget must be to define what the organisation's objectives are. We might believe that most commercial enterprises have the primary objective of maximising returns to their owners or, in other words, maximising profit. However, even the most profit driven organisations have to ensure that both cash and risk are also managed; if they do not, then shareholders may lose all their money when the organisation goes bust.

Commercial organisations should normally seek to maximise profit in the long run. To do this they may well set other secondary objectives such as achieving certain levels of market share, developing new products and developing staff capabilities or new technologies.

Managers need to be aware not only of an organisation's objectives, but also its strategy, values, policies and plans (see Chapter 9 for more on these).

Equally, managers in 'not-for-profit' organisations need to understand the organisation's objectives and what the key performance measures are when building and managing budgets. Not-for-profit organisations often have a range of primary objectives which have to be balanced within the budgeting process.

Budgets should be linked to objectives and strategy. In order for this to be done, objectives and strategy need to be communicated to budget holders when they are building and managing their budgets. A mechanism which may help is the balanced scorecard and strategy maps (developed by Professor Robert Kaplan and Dr David Norton). (There will be greater coverage of balanced scorecards and strategy maps later in the book – see Chapter 9.)

Exercise

1 List out the values and primary objectives for your organisation and department. Make a note of how these objectives could influence how you go about building or managing a budget.

2 Describe the strategy for your organisation. How do you seek to achieve your organisational objectives and beat the competition? How does this strategy influence how you build and manage budgets?

3 If you are in a senior role in the organisation, how do you effectively communicate the organisation's objectives and strategy to budget holders?

2 Planning

The budget can act as a plan to help us to achieve our objectives. In fact, in many US organisations, the budget is often referred to as the annual operating plan. Using this description may give us a rather more precise view of the budget and help change people's attitudes to it.

Thinking of the budget as primarily being a plan gives us a different view and probably a different approach when we start to construct and manage it. If a budget is a plan, it should be a costed version of what we are going to do over the year. When we review performance, we must review differences in what actually happened against the original plan. You cannot plan for every eventuality, so you should not expect to be spot on with your budget. In fact budget performance with no variances (differences between the actual results and the budget or plan) should perhaps be viewed with some suspicion.

Producing a costed plan may be easier for some elements of the budget than others. For some minor activities or elements there may be little to be gained from trying to cost the budget out in too much detail. Always seek to consolidate small costs or sundry items into fewer lines in the budget.

Producing a costed plan: illustration

The maintenance department in an engineering company could put together a plan of work for preventative maintenance across the year. It would also need to make an estimate of likely reactive maintenance and how much that may cost.

Managers often believe that uncertain things cannot be planned or budgeted for. We do however know that there will be unforeseen events and costs that will need to be managed cost effectively. The maintenance manager might put in a contingency for reactive or unplanned maintenance. When some plant fails he or she will need to manage the cost of repairing it and explain why it failed in the first place. There is more detail on how you can build a budget to cover expected events or for contingencies in Chapter 4.

Exercise

1 List out the work that your department is expected to carry out. Identify what work can be predicted and planned with a high degree of certainty and what cannot.

2 How do you budget for work that cannot be planned in detail?

3 How might you attempt to set up and manage a contingency?

3 Monitoring and controlling

In a lot of organisations, managers and many accountants too, tend to focus on the control aspects of budgets and budgeting. It is important to remember that in order to control costs, income and cash, we need to start with a good plan, against which we can monitor our performance.

By monitoring our financial performance, we do not control it, but at the same time it is very difficult to control without monitoring. How often and in what detail should income and cost be monitored? This partly depends upon the nature of the income costs and how they are likely to change. In most organisations, variances from budget are produced every month with major variations from budget requiring an explanation. It is tempting to suggest that all variances outside a tolerance limit – say 10 per cent under or over spent – should be investigated. It would be better to focus on a few key figures that make up most of the budget. Small costs may be difficult to budget for and ultimately they have little impact on the budget.

Rather than controlling solely through the budget (a lagging indicator – an indicator of what has already happened) managers can monitor other figures that lead expenditure or income. These could be items such as overtime hours or forward customer orders taken. The earlier that feedback (or feed-forward – indicators telling us what is likely to happen) can be obtained, the greater the number of opportunities managers have to take corrective action. Feed-forward can be developed further by producing reforecasts to compare against the original budget.

Major underspends should always be monitored and explained just like overspends. An underspend today might result in an overspend later if we are merely delaying expenditure. Underspends that are due to cost saving measures should be indentified and promoted to other parts of the organisation.

When we review our performance we might assume that the budget is always right, but sometimes budgets do have errors, such as sections of expenditure being missed out. Also several factors may have changed since the original budget was drawn up. It is tempting to update the budget to reflect these errors or changes, but it is important to keep the budget fixed as a marker to measure our performance against. We may however update the forecast. The forecast is the latest estimate of how the current year's figures will turn out. In some organisations it is known as the latest estimate. It is important to differentiate between the budget and the forecast and there is more on forecasting in the next chapter.

Exercise

1   What are the key lines (accounts or types of expenditure) of your budget that make up the majority of your costs or expenditure?

2 Can you indentify any leading indicators for each, which will give you some early warning signs that something might be straying from your original plan?

4 Co-ordinating

The act of putting together budgets helps us to coordinate the activities of different parts of the organisation. The budgets and plans need to fit and work together. Different departments' and units' plans need to make the best use of the organisation's limited resources (known as the limiting factors).

All departments need to be consistent in order to drive the organisation in the same direction. When organisations put together budgets for individual departments this should be done within an overall plan. The overall plan needs to take into account its strategy and priorities. Without adequate co-ordination, budgets can easily lose their strategic focus.

Examples of budget links

■ The sales budget might be driven by profit performance targets.

■ The production budget might be driven by the sales budget.

■ The personnel budget might be driven by the production plan.

■ The training budget might be driven by the personnel plan.

■ The customer service skills development training budget might be driven by a marketing plan.

Exercise

1 What do you think should be the starting point for budgets in your organisation? Do you think it should be profit, sales, production/delivery capacity or something else?

2 What drives your department's budgets? What is the starting point? What *should be* the starting point?

When building budgets we should always refer back to our objectives. For many large quoted businesses, the objective is about satisfying shareholder objectives, which generally means achieving a certain level of profit for today. We should also remember that shareholders want a profit today *and* tomorrow. Budgets should be about ensuring that the organisation is equipped to deliver the return shareholders expect in the medium and longer term.

Organisations should define what they need to be delivering today to be able to deliver tomorrow. For example, we may set targets and goals around employee development and product development today to ensure we deliver the profits shareholders want for tomorrow. This also applies to not-for-profit organisations. Most charities will set a budget to aim to make a small surplus – the surplus today ensures that the charity can grow to deliver more tomorrow. If you build your budget based around your objectives and then discover a limiting factor (a constraint preventing you from delivering it) you must then focus on that constraint and try to manage it. Co-ordination through the organisation should help to identify limiting factors or constraints in other departments.

5 Evaluating performance

We may use budgets to judge the performance of individual units within the organisation and to judge the performance of managers. It should be remembered that performance should also be measured in terms other than just the performance against the budget. For example, a department manager may underspend his or her budget but deliver poor performance in terms of the output of the department. Perhaps budgets should be judged in conjunction with other KPIs.

Managers should be measured on what they control. For example a retail manager may be held generally accountable for the profit in his or her store, but not accountable for the profit margin changes that result from actions by the firm's buyers.

Often cost and profitability are affected by teams of people working across different departments and functions. The performance measurement aspect of a budget may encourage managers to retreat into their own departmental 'silos' and focus on what is good for them and their unit, rather than what is good for the organisation.

Measuring a manager's performance based upon his or her budget may encourage managers to negotiate their budgets to make it easier for them to achieve rather than aiming to maximise the performance of their unit. This problem is known as the dysfunctional behavioural aspect of budgeting and is one of the reasons put forward for scrapping budgets (or adopting 'beyond budgeting' – see Chapter 11). You are probably not in a position to take such a radical step in your organisation. It may be that budgets can never be perfect, so how else could we remove or lessen this dysfunctional aspect of budgeting?

Potential remedies to think about are as follows:

■ Design performance measures that encourage managers to work with corporate interests in mind. Such measures encourage them to deliver corporate objectives and stakeholders' needs. Match managers' goals with the organisation's goals – this is known as goal congruence. (Related tools and approaches to help organisations create this goal congruence are Kaplan and Norton's balanced scorecard and EVA – economic value added.[1]

■ Include performance measures or KPIs beyond the budget including measures which look outside the organisation. Do not aim to set fixed internal targets, but set targets of relative performance against peer companies and the 'best in class'.

■ Encourage managers to indentify and report opportunities to serve the organisation's and stakeholders' interests better.

Exercise

1 Can you indentify an occasion when the building and delivery of budgets in your organisation did not serve the interests of the organisation or its stakeholders?

2 In those instances, why do you think the budgetary control system failed?

3 What could have been done differently to reduce the chances of failure happening then or in the future?

6 Improving performance

Budgets are sometimes seen as targets to beat to deliver improved performance. If the budget is a target it should be set carefully. If the budget is too challenging, managers may be de-motivated; if it is too easy they will not strive to do their best.

---

1 EVA is a registered trade mark of the consulting firm Stern Stewart & Co: **www.sternstewart.com**.

Rather than encouraging managers to deliver their best performance, budgets may be incentivised, thus motivating them to deliver only 'satisfactory' performance – just meeting the target. An annual fixed performance target symptomatic of a traditional budget encourages managers to negotiate their target downwards to make success easier rather than to seek improvements.

The remedy is to put in some additional measures beyond the budget that include continuous improvement targets (such as reducing unit costs) or relative performance (how we compare against our competition or other organisations similar to ours).

Performance benchmarking

Budgets normally focus on annual performance based on the organisation's financial year. This pressure to focus on the financial year is strongest in stock market quoted businesses that have to deliver results to keep shareholders satisfied. Ideally managers should also be focused on performance over the long term – a good profit this year can be at the expense of next year's profit. A 12-month rolling average compared to previous years should give an indication if things are getting better or worse. Rolling forecasts of 12 to 24 months should encourage managers to focus on a longer-term horizon. (Further details about rolling forecasts are covered in the next chapter.)

It is important not to rely on performance against budget as a sole measure of performance. Organisations also need to develop *relevant* KPIs for both the organisation and for individual departments. The kind of indicators to look out for are:

■ market share

■ total shareholder returns (TSRs) compared to peer companies[2]

■ level of customer satisfaction compared to peer group companies.

You can also use benchmarking to compare the performance of individual departments. For example, you might compare the finance department's performance against its budget but also benchmark the

---

2 The TSR is a combination of the dividend and the growth in share price, and comparisons of TSR are presented in the accounts of major quoted businesses. The TSR for a period = (share price at end of period – share price at beginning of period + Dividends)/share price at the beginning of the period.

costs of the department against the costs of the finance department in other organisations.

The practice of benchmarking was developed in the early 1980s. It has its origins in the Xerox Company's 'Leadership through Quality' programme. Xerox discovered that its competitors were selling photocopiers at a lower price than Xerox was manufacturing them for. The average manufacturing cost of photocopiers in Japanese companies was estimated at 40–50 per cent of that of Xerox.

Xerox then engaged in a programme of cost reduction that included extensive benchmarking. There are a number of benchmarking organisations and benchmarking syndicates where companies share information on costs. Within this book we provide some information from the Hackett Group which provides benchmarking information for finance departments.

Benchmarking is a continuous improvement process, which in many organisations has been superseded. More recent continuous improvement models are Six Sigma and lean manufacturing.

7 Motivating managers

Managers may be motivated to perform since they are being judged against a budget. It may be that the budgetary control systems actually motivate managers in the wrong direction (as described previously). They may be incentivised to spend their budgets if they believe they may be cut if they do not. They may be incentivised to try to increase their cost budget and reduce income budgets to make their performance targets easier. Again the solution is to develop performance measures that go beyond the budget and encourage managers to focus on beating the competition.

A manager's approach to delegating budgets will be influenced by how he or she views staff and perceives how they are motivated. Some managers believe staff are motivated to 'do the right thing' for the organisation and as such they require little supervision when it comes to managing budgets. Other managers believe staff will pursue their own personal interests and therefore it makes little sense for them to be delegating budgets; if they do they may end up 'micromanaging' their staff.

8 A management contract

Ideally, a budget should be seen as a contract between the manager and the organisation. The contract should cover what the manager will deliver at what cost and this will be negotiated and agreed with the line manager. The negotiation element of the budget is criticised by the advocates of 'beyond budgeting' (the approach that recommends scrapping budgets). The negotiation encourages game playing, where managers are incentivised to try to make their budgets and targets easier to achieve.

In most organisations the 'game' is recognised – budget reviewers and senior managers should review budgets with an understanding of the individuals that build them and set targets beyond the budget, including external benchmarks.

9 Communicating

A key to effective budgeting must be good communication. It could be argued that the budget itself is a form of communication. Budgets inform managers and employees of the plans and strategy of the organisation expressed in financial terms.

In the budget setting process, senior managers will set goals and targets. Budget managers must then construct their budgets within those requirements and the constraints of their departments. This process gives them an opportunity to give senior managers feedback on what is and what is not possible.

Budgets operate differently in different organisations. In some organisations, feedback or communication is valued yet in others the budget setting process does not seek feedback and is more of an instruction.

Exercise

1 How are details of budgets and targets communicated within your organisation?

2 How could this communication be improved?

3 What actions can you take to improve communication about budgets and targets in your organisation?

10 Providing a basis for authorising expenditure and delegating responsibility

It is important to provide a basis for authorising expenditure and delegating authority and responsibility. Budgets fail when authority and responsibility are not matched. When an organisation gives a manager a budget, it is delegating authority.

Budgets may be delegated through responsibility centres, these are usually called cost centres or profit centres, a rather rarer term is investment centres.

In a cost centre, a manager is made responsible for cost. He or she should also be made responsible for delivering some output or outcome. Cost centres and their managers should not be measured on the costs alone, but should also be measured against appropriate KPIs. An approach that might be adopted in a cost centre is a variation on the value for money or VFM model (further details of this model and approach are in Chapter 7).

Profit centre managers are responsible for income and costs and can be more legitimately measured purely on the bottom line or net profit. Profit centre managers often have responsibilities beyond delivering a profit – an example would be maintaining brand standards or complying with health and safety legislation.

Organisations sometimes make cost centres more like profit centres by introducing internal charges and service level agreements (SLAs) between departments. Some of our clients have elegantly described these cost centres as 'cost recovery centres': they do not make a profit and aim to break even from their charges. Internal charges may help to allocate resources better but may also cause extra work and internal disputes.

An investment centre might be a business unit where a manager is responsible for income cost and investment – the manager and his or her unit might be measured in terms of return on capital employed (ROCE) or return on investment (ROI).

Summary of responsibility centres

- Cost centre and departments that incur costs with no external income.
- Cost recovery centre – costs are recovered in internal charges.
- Profit centre – incurs costs and earns real income: can be measured in terms of profit or loss.
- Investment centre – a profit centre with an allocation investment or capital employed: can be measured and targeted in terms of ROCE or ROI.

A challenge for many organisations is to assign responsibility. It may be that the costs or profits cannot truly be the responsibility of one manager in one area but are the result of many managers' decisions in different departments. A heavy emphasis on cost responsibility may make some managers overprotective of their budgets, as they are concerned about their own performance evaluation above the organisation's performance. Budget managers with organisational objectives should be given priority in decision making.

11 Identifying scarce resources

The process of building a budget may help us to identify scarce resources and resources that need to be managed carefully or increased. All organisations have constraints, bottlenecks or limiting factors. For example, a factory will have a limited production capacity, a call centre has a defined capacity. Building a budget requires us to indentify these constraints, to manage them and to optimise them.

Building a budget for an organisation may take much negotiation and result in many iterations or rounds. This can easily result in mistakes being made around capacity estimates and the use of limiting factors. The solution is to cut down the iterations thereby reducing the chances of errors and speeding up the process. According to a study by the Hackett Group in 2011[3], the most successful companies tend to start with a strong top-down approach.

Budgeting at a strategic level must also consider longer-term capacity planning. Building too little capacity constrains the organisation; building too much leads to needless extra cost and suboptimal operations.

Exercise

1   List out the main limiting factors in your organisation.
2   What are the constraints which will govern the limits for your organisation's budget?
3   What could you do to ensure that these limiting factors are best utilised to maximise your returns?

---

3 Enterprise Performance Management Research Series, The Hackett Group, 2008–2011.

12 Allocating resources

Budgets may be used to allocate resources, sometimes based on a formula. For example a major UK police force developed a formula to divide a pre-defined budget between geographic areas. The formula was derived from one used by the Home Office to divide the national budget between police forces. The formula took into account a number of factors to try to determine the relative policing demand within different geographic areas. This approach appears fair and removes all the problems of negotiation, but it also moves the budget away from building a plan of what managers are actually going to do and what they are going to achieve. Generally, formulae for budget allocations are wrong – fully costed plans with quantified targeted for outputs, outputs or expected results are much better.

Example of using a formula

Training budgets are often calculated as an allowance per employee. Initially this looks like a fair formula, but is it the best way to set a budget? Organisations often want to encourage relevant training and this method of setting the budget may just encourage spending on training but without perhaps enough consideration of whether the training is useful or relevant.

A manager may book an expensive training course at the end of the year just to use up the budget, and justify next year's budget. Better motivated and organised managers will plan their training to maximise its return. They may still aim to spend every penny of it though, as there is no incentive for making a saving and they may still believe they will be penalised next year with a smaller budget. To reduce this harmful thinking budgets should be promoted and treated as plans that are not dependent upon the previous year's spending.

When selling training to potential clients, we have often encountered the words 'we cannot have the training, there is nothing in the budget' or 'we can have the training – there is money in the budget': in other words, the judgement about training is based upon a budget allocation rather than on a training plan. Spending should be driven by need and benefit, not by budget allocation. Therefore budgets should be built based upon need and benefit.

A training budget should be built around training plans based on what training needs to be delivered to meet the organisation's objectives. If savings are required, across the board percentage cuts to all allocated budget may seem fair, but are in fact arbitrary – the training budget in one area may be more significant to the overall performance of the business than the training budget in another area. Cutting equally might not be best for the organisation aiming to achieve its objectives.

Budget cuts should be deliberate – it may be better to cut all the training in just one area rather than employ the same across the board reductions. A budget based on planned activity should make this decision clearer, as a budget cut would mean cutting a planned activity.

Exercise

In the above example we have focused on the training budget. Now try to think about your own organisation and budgets.

1   Are any budgets in your organisation allocated by a formula?

2   Why are these formulae used?

3   How else could these budgets be better built?

4   Have you experienced people trying to use up this year's budget to justify next year's budget?

5   How could you change this behaviour?

6   Has your organisation ever imposed arbitrary or blanket cuts? Examples of arbitrary budget cuts are: 5 per cent of all budgets; a ban on foreign flights or other restrictions on travel; a freeze on advertising and promotion.

7   How should cuts be made? (In Chapter 7 we make suggestions about making savings out of your budget.)

13 Demonstrating and delivering good corporate governance

The budgetary control system is effectively part of the internal control system within an organisation. It could be argued that organisations only need this internal control because they are delegating financial control (or budgets) to managers, so it is not really a function of a budget. Whatever your view, delivering corporate governance does affect our approach to budgets.

Increasingly, organisations are required to demonstrate that they have systems to ensure good corporate governance. Corporate governance is about ensuring that the managers of the company look after the interests of the stakeholders in the organisation (in quoted businesses, normally the shareholders).

In 2002, after a number of high-profile accounting and business scandals in the US (Enron and WorldCom) the US government passed a law known as the Sarbanes–Oxley Act, SOX or Sarbox (named after the sponsors US Senator Paul Sarbanes and US Representative Michael G. Oxley).

The act required companies to demonstrate they had sufficient corporate governance through adequate financial controls and procedures. The new law also covered all US companies and non-US companies with a US stockmarket listing. Sarbanes–Oxley led to some companies making budget management and control more formalised and rule bound. For example, partly as a result of Sarbanes–Oxley, one UK bank intro-duced a new system requiring all managers to formally check their cost centre (department) financial reports at the end of each month and to sign electronically to say they were happy to accept responsibility that the costs were correctly recorded. The system then automatically highlighted managers who were not complying with this check.

To reinforce the system, the bank trained the majority of cost centre managers in the new system. Some of the bank's accountants resisted the implementation of this system believing it to be a threat to their role from the corporate centre. Some cost centre managers rather foolishly saw it as an administrative 'tick box' exercise and probably signed the report without a thorough check.

There are business benefits to requiring managers to conduct such checks. We suggest to companies that they encourage managers to conduct genuine checks on significant costs on their cost centre or profit centre reports. In doing this, some of our clients have found mistakes (including being overcharged by suppliers), savings and improved performance. We believe you should always check your personal shopping and restaurant receipts and bills – overcharges are rare, but you will discover some.

Doubts over the strengths of a company's system for ensuring corporate governance and maintaining financial control may adversely affect its value. In September 2011 a rogue London trader (Kweku Adoboli) in the Swiss bank UBS revealed he had lost the bank £1.3 billion through alleged unauthorised transactions without sufficient hedges (a mechanism to cover the bank's risks – banks, like bookmakers, are not supposed to gamble). The result was a review by all three major ratings agencies – Moody's, Standard & Poor's and Fitch – of the bank's credit rating. *The Daily Telegraph* (on 15 September 2011) indicated at the time that the scandal wiped £4 billion off UBS's value.

Enron, WorldCom and Barings were all thought to have operated within tight financial controls and were 'driven by the numbers'

– but ultimately their control systems failed to protect shareholders' interests.

Linking budgets to strategy and policy

If a budget is a plan then it should be linked to the business strategy. We cannot build budgets without first understanding what our strategies are. We cannot manage budgets without understanding our strategy; we would not be able to make judgements about cutting costs in pursuing income unless we knew that these actions were in line with the company's strategy, policy and objectives. Many large organisations do not integrate budgets with their strategy; some do not really have a strategy.

Business strategy can seem remote for junior managers managing a small budget but if they are to be effective, it is important that they understand the bigger picture. Organisations should seek to communicate their strategy to all managers so that they can make their decisions in a way which is consistent with the company's strategy. A mechanism to link budgets to strategy is the balanced scorecard and strategy map. Budgets should also be consistent with the organisation's values, mission and vision. (Values, mission and vision, the balance scorecard and strategy maps are covered in Chapter 9.)

Do you know what your company strategy is, and should you?

Strategy is often seen as something that should be kept secret, only senior managers having access to the details. Yet in order for a strategy to be delivered effectively it needs to be communicated throughout the organisation.

Budgets for special purposes

You may need to put forward a budget for a special purpose, such as raising finance for a business or a project. If you are doing this, start with a clear idea of your objectives and what the barriers will be to achieving them.

If we are trying to raise funds from investors we have to be truthful but must also aim to present a convincing plan that fills them with confidence and addresses their potential concerns. A good business plan or business case is often critical to gaining investment. Very often it is more about the confidence the reviewers have in the people who will be delivering the plan. A good plan and a good presentation do not guarantee that the reviewers will be filled with confidence, but a poor plan or a poor presentation is likely to diminish their confidence.

Planning periods

Generally, when we think about budgets we think about the annual plan. Plans can be put together over short- or longer-term periods. How long term you can plan for will depend very much upon your business and the industry in which it operates. In many industries long-term planning is becoming increasingly difficult as markets and technology have become much more volatile; all plans have thus had to become more flexible. Many major companies produce three- or five-year plans; in some industries such as utilities they may well produce plans that run over several decades. Most of the smaller businesses we work with often find it difficult to plan more than a year ahead.

·Plan strategy
look at budgeting – business need + benefit
Communicate strategy to manager

2

What is a forecast and how does it differ from a budget?

What is the difference between a budget and a forecast? What is the function of a forecast? What tools and techniques are available? How frequently should forecasts be produced and how can we make them more accurate and more useful? These questions are addressed in this chapter.

What is the difference between a budget and a forecast?

Budgets describe what the future is most likely to look like (based upon our plans); forecasts describe what the budget is most likely to look like.

Forecasts as updates to the annual budget

Managers often confuse budgets and forecasts. When the budget is produced it may require some forecasting to derive some of the figures. 'The forecast' is an updated estimate of the outturn or result for the year. In most large organisations a reforecast is normally produced every quarter or every month. The process of reforecasting encourages managers to rethink how the year's result is going to develop; this may enable them to identify problems sooner and become more proactive and less reactive when managing the budget.

It is generally seen as good practice to keep the original budget intact and use it as a fixed benchmark to measure performance against

– changing the original budget would be confusing when relating performance against budget.

The tools and techniques for the construction of forecasts are covered in the second half of this chapter.

Rolling forecasts

Forecasts can also be produced on a rolling basis beyond the end of the current financial year – perhaps always looking forward over the next 12 or 18 months. The time period that you should be forecasting will depend upon your company and the industry. In some industries forecasting over more than three months is a challenge, others may be able to make effective forecasts over several years (and we have suggested some examples below). The increase in uncertainty is a factor that actually makes the process of forecasting more important as we need to detect problems as early as possible.

Industries and functions that should have shorter rolling forecasts

Industries	Retailing
	Consumer electronics
Functions	Advertising and promotion

Industries and functions that may have longer rolling forecasts

Industries	Oil exploration
	Utilities – infrastructure investment
	Pharmaceuticals
Functions	Research and development (R&D)

A good guide when considering how frequently forecasts should be redone and in what detail is to consider the variability and impact of the change, as shown in the following table.

		Variability	
		Low	**High**
Impact (consequence of variation)	**High**	Medium frequency (monthly or quarterly)	Frequent and routine (weekly or even daily) – forecast only over a short period
	Low	Least frequent and maybe even just 'event driven' – reforecast only made after significant events. Forecast over a long period	Medium frequency (monthly or quarterly)

For example, consider the impact and volatility of fuel prices on an airline. These may need to be managed and reforecast weekly or even daily whereas the cost of leasing the aircraft is long term and fairly static. The fuel price forecast may be as short as a single month while the forecast for the lease cost of the aircraft may run over several years.

Benefits of forecasting 'beyond the wall'

Often organisations focus solely on the problems of the current year's budget as they are driven to meet shareholder requirements for the current financial year. (This tends to be less of a problem in small private organisations.) The shareholders should be interested not only in the current year's performance, but also future years' performance.

Forecasting solely to the year-end reinforces short-term thinking. In order to deliver the best returns to shareholders it is better to look over a much longer timescale. It is almost as if the year-end is viewed as a wall that we cannot see over. On the other side of 'the wall' there may be some big risks to manage.

The addition of a rolling forecast encourages managers to think beyond the current year and to try to predict potential problems well before they happen. If they can do this they can then manage those risks.

Rolling forecasts enable managers to reduce their reliance on budgets. They are often a fundamental part of a new approach that aims to do away with budgets ('beyond budgeting' is covered in detail in Chapter 11).

The 'beyond budgeting' approach advocates getting rid of the budget, often putting an emphasis on rolling forecasts. Even within businesses that still adhere to more traditional ideas of budgeting there is considerable benefit to be gained from producing rolling forecasts.

According to a study by the Hackett Group in 2008[1], companies that produced rolling forecasts were able to produce their annual budgets much faster, more accurately and were viewed as being much more satisfactory.

Should forecasts be produced 'top-down' or 'bottom-up'? ('Top-down' means that directives come from the top or board level whereas 'bottom-up' is more driven by departments.) Top-down forecasts can be produced more quickly but may miss some vital detail of changes happening within the business, and ultimately figures need to come from the business not the finance function. The sales forecast should be produced by the sales department. Production forecasts should then be produced by the production department in the light of the sales forecast.

The best compromise may be to develop a co-ordinated forecast that connects with key information from the business. Forecasts have to be simple, quick, easy, cost-effective and useful. Simple key elements to focus on might be sales, gross margins, variable costs and fixed costs.

Ideally the production of forecasts should be automated as much as possible, with financial figures in the forecast being generated from existing operational data within the company. Some figures can be generated from 'actuals': for example sales orders may be the basis for next month's forecast sales.

Rolling forecasts may be produced either monthly or quarterly and their frequency will depend upon the rate of change within the organisation. However frequently you reforecast, it also makes sense to take into account major events. A major change in your market or your costs may warrant a reforecast.

Following the global economic crisis of 2008, many organisations found their original budgets to be out of date and redundant. This meant instead that they had to rely on using frequently updated forecasts. Updating the rolling forecast too frequently is wasteful of resources; for most organisations a quarterly update is probably adequate.

---

1 Enterprise Performance Management Research Series, The Hackett Group, 2008–2011.

In many organisations, rolling forecasts, if produced at all, are produced with internally designed spreadsheet models. These models typically have a number of problems:

- poor version control – confusion arises from several versions of the forecast being produced
- a high proportion of logic errors (mistakes in spreadsheet formulae)
- poor spreadsheet design (spreadsheets not typically produced by professional programmers)
- difficulty in updating and revising assumptions and being unable to accommodate changes easily
- overall models may be made up of a patchwork of spreadsheets around the business which users might change, making the model weak, flawed and prone to breakdowns
- the end result frequently lacks credibility in the eyes of senior managers
- models are difficult to audit
- data security may be compromised as information is distributed on easily copied and emailed spreadsheets.

Some of these weaknesses may be overcome with some controls. There are further notes on potential solutions to these problems and improving spreadsheets' design and use at the end of Chapter 4.

Exercise

1 Review the use of spreadsheets in your own organisation for forecasts or budgets.
2 Do any of the above listed problems arise?
3 What measures could you or your organisation take to reduce them?

In large organisations, a solution to these problems is to purchase a dedicated 'black box' planning and forecasting software tool, and there are a number of competing packages, for example Cognos Express Planner from IBM.

Many software companies produce 'white papers' describing the best practice for rolling forecasts – naturally the white paper usually concludes with the author company's solution being the best! Some resistance to purchased solutions may come from members of the finance team who *create one template?*

have developed Excel skills and spend a large proportion of their time working on spreadsheets. Whatever solution you use to build your rolling forecasts, make sure it is simple for all users.

One might believe the most useful forecasts are the most accurate. Forecasts though can never be totally accurate. It is more important that forecasts provide some valuable management insight into what is happening so that the organisation can respond. If your forecasting approach is not helping you to manage, then scrap it or change it. If it is working well for you, you can still work on improvements.

When you have developed a good approach to producing forecasts you can also use them to test out different scenarios. These might be for different decisions within your business. An example could be changing product launch dates or may be about different expectations of external factors such as the marketplace.

Forecasts, projects and contracts

If you are working on a project or a contract, you could forecast to its end. This approach might help you identify problems earlier.

Reviewing the project just on its performance to date may make you complacent. It is important to remember that the sooner you identify a problem the more solutions you will have to solve it. Projects or contracts may well appear to be under budget but are actually just behind schedule. If you produce a reforecast up to a project's full completion, it should then eliminate this mistake.

When producing the forecast you need to remember the matrix of impact and variability described earlier. What are the key factors that are most likely to change and have a significant impact on the project?

Review questions

1 Do you or your finance department produce regular reforecasts?

2 How could the forecast and forecasting process be improved? (Improvement would relate to more useful information or that the forecast is simpler and/or quicker to produce.)

3 Do you or your organisation use rolling forecasts? If you do, how are they produced and could their production be improved? If you do not, do you think they would be useful?

4   What do you think the forecast horizon should be for your department or organisation? Three months, 12 months, 18 months?

5   Which figures are the most important ones for you to forecast to improve decision making within your department or organisation?

6   Review the reports that your finance department produces for you: can you differentiate between the budget and a forecast?

Reviewing your reforecasting frequency and length (how many months the forecast stretches into the future)

List out your organisation's main costs and income, and score each in terms of its variability and the impact of its change. Then review how often you or your organisation reforecast them and how far you forecast them into the future. Remember, highly variable, high-impact items will generally require more frequent, regular, shorter forecasts.

Forecasting tools and techniques

Within the business there are a variety of figures which may be forecasted including:

- sales
- profit and loss
- cash flow.

In 2011, the Hackett Group undertook a study[2] to try to gauge the accuracy of firms' forecasts of sales, profit (earnings) and cash flow. The study also examined how accurate short-term forecasts were in comparison to longer-term forecasts. The results are shown in Table 2.1.

The conclusion from the study is that the best companies are much better at forecasting for sales, earnings and cash flow. The decline

---

2 Enterprise Performance Management Research Series, The Hackett Group, 2008–2011.

table 2.1	Forecast accuracy (based on 200 major companies)		
		Top performers (%)	Peer group (%)
Sales	One month	4	7
	One quarter	4	8
	More than one quarter	5	9
Earnings	One month	4	8
	One quarter	5	10
	More than one quarter	8	11
Cash	One month	8	16
	One quarter	9	16
	More than one quarter	10	16

Source: Enterprise Performance Management Research Series, The Hackett Group, 2008–2011

in forecast accuracy with longer-term forecasts is surprisingly small. Cash flow forecasts are the least accurate; in many companies they are probably inadequate.

The best way to produce a forecast and its required predictive accuracy will depend upon exactly why the forecast is required. In many businesses and industries, forecasting is likely to become more difficult with changing, disruptive technology and a changing economic and social environment. It is never possible to produce a 100 per cent accurate forecast so organisations should be seeking to produce forecasts that are useful.

— to Do — targets for sales

Sales forecasting

Q for the FC — which are limited by capacity?

In many businesses, the starting point for a budget or plan will be the expected or potential sales. Sales may be limited by production or service capacity constraints. They will also be determined by customer demand, competitor action, economic circumstances and the possibility of substitutes (customers buying alternative products or services to meet their demands). This complex mix makes sales forecasting sound impossible, yet some organisations manage to forecast with a surprising degree of accuracy.

There are two main broad approaches to producing a forecast:

1 **Quantitative** – this approach is based upon statistical analysis. The analysis is done typically by looking at past data. Many

companies using quantitative techniques will produce forecasts using Microsoft Excel. The Excel package is almost universally used and the standard version includes a number of data analysis tools, including tools specifically designed for producing forecasts. Additional statistical functions can be added via various 'add-ins'.

2 **Qualitative** – this approach is based upon opinion and judgement. In many organisations, sales forecasts will be generated by sales and marketing professionals, trying to make judgements about market demand and how much market share the company can win.

   In some instances salespeople may be able to identify potential upcoming orders and contracts and assign a probability of winning them. Sales in the very near future can often be predicted very accurately as a customer may have already placed an order although it may not have been delivered.

   When people produce forecasts they often have their own agendas. For example, sales managers may be reluctant to propose an ambitious sales forecast if they believe they are subsequently going to be judged against this figure.

   If a team was created to produce a sales forecast, each member of the team might be influenced by the general opinion of the team. This problem can be eliminated by using a technique called Delphi. In the Delphi technique, experts are quizzed independently to give their views about the forecast; this then reduces the chance of a group bias effect.

   No point in/or or over exaggeraty

   Forecasts can also be subject to 'political' bias. For example, managers at all levels may be tempted to adjust or influence the figures to match their own requirements. Forecasts of bad news might be seen as being almost disloyal to the organisation. Truthful attempts at forecasts are always best and an organisation's leadership should promote a culture that encourages this.

   Both market research and test marketing may give information and data to assist in building more objective sales forecasts.

However you go about producing your forecasts, it is important to test them. To do this, ask yourself the following questions:

■ How accurate are they?

■ How accurate do they need to be?

✳ ■ Are the forecasts useful?

■ How could we make the forecasts more accurate?

■ How could we make the forecasts more useful?

You could try different approaches to produce your forecasts and then compare the results against a few months of actual performance in a 'tournament of techniques'. Then try to make a judgement about which technique is right for you and your organisation in the current circumstances.

The Delphi technique and forecasting

The Delphi technique is a structured approach to bringing together the estimates of a number of experts, without each of the experts inadvertently or deliberately influencing the others' views. The technique was developing by the RAND Corporation for the US military in the 1940s. The US wanted to forecast the technology that a potential enemy might use against it in the future. Using the Delphi technique a team of experts is assembled. They are asked independently for their views in the form of answers to a questionnaire. This stops people being swayed by the views of other experts. The results are collected by a facilitator who identifies consensus and disagreement. The group is given feedback on the results of the questionnaire and the experts may then amend their predictions. The process is repeated until sufficient consensus is reached.

Exercise

Think about your own organisation. How could you structure the pooling of expert opinions within your organisation to make it more like the Delphi technique?

Quantitative forecasting using Microsoft Excel

Quantitative techniques give the illusion of factual accuracy. All models (even Microsoft Excel models) have estimates and assumptions behind them. Excel models often include errors and the data behind the model may be inaccurate, incomplete or even estimated. Quantitative forecasts involve building a model, normally based on historical data. Our model may fit the historical data perfectly. This perfect fit may persuade some people that the model's predictive accuracy is going to be very high but it is important to note that the past is never a perfect mirror of the future.

Widely used quantitative forecasting techniques include:

- moving averages
- weighted moving averages

■ exponential smoothing

■ regression analysis.

Generally these techniques work by using assumptions that base future forecasts on past results and figures. For example, the simplest way of forecasting the weather is to say that the weather tomorrow will be the same as the weather today (this is known as a *naive forecast*, also discussed below). Statistically this technique may well give a fairly accurate forecast. It is probably better though to forecast by including other data in the analysis, such as seasonal and historical data, together with information about wind speeds, air pressure and precipitation.

These models use historical data as the starting point. For example, a sales forecast will be built on the basis of previous months' sales. Within our historical sales we may have some months where the sales pattern has been corrupted by external factors. Before we start to build a model we will have to clean up our data, taking out the 'blips'. Factors that may affect the sales pattern include supply shortages holding back sales, promotional activity bringing forward sales and competitor promotional activity dampening sales.

Naive forecast

The simplest forecast is known as a naive forecast. This is where you simply take the last period's figures and say that the forecast for the current period will be the same.

Example: actual sales January–March

Month	Sales	Naive forecast
January	900	
February	1,200	900
March	1,500	1,200
April (Forecast)		1,500

Moving averages

A moving average forecasts the current period based on the average of a number of previous periods. A variation on this is to assign different weights to the previous periods.

Example: a three-month moving average

Forecast sales for April = (900 + 1,200 + 1,500) / 3 = 1,200

Weighted moving averages

A weighted moving average assigns different weights to each period within the calculation.

Example: a three-month weighted moving average

Month	Sales A	Weight B	A × B
January	900	0.2	180
February	1,200	0.3	360
March	1,500	0.5	750
April (Forecast)			1,290

Different weightings could be tested to see which gives the best forecast result.

Exponential smoothing

Exponential smoothing is a method that looks at how accurate a previous forecast was against what actually happened. You take the difference and take a proportion (known as the alpha, which is set between 0 and 1) of this error and add it to the previous forecast to derive the current forecast.

Example: alpha = 0.3

Month	Sales	Forecast	Difference from actual
January	900		
February	1,200	900	300
March	1,500	900 + (300 x 0.3) = 990	510
April (Forecast)		990 + (510 x 0.3) = 1,143	

If alpha is set at 1 then the result would be the same as the naive forecast taking no account of actual results before the last period. If alpha is set at zero then the forecast would be unchanged from the first forecast.

This method of forecasting is widely used and is a good method when there is no pattern or trend in the actual figures. If there is a pattern, regression analysis may be a better technique.

Regression analysis

Regression analysis uses one variable (the independent variable x) to predict another (the dependent variable y). In the simplest form of regression analysis there is a linear or straight line relationship (see Figure 2.1), described by the simple formula:

$$y = a + bx$$

Using a series of data for x and y we can see that there is likely to be a relation between the two, and calculate the 'best fit' to estimate a (the intercept) and b (the slope).

A common mistake when using regression analysis is to confuse a correlation with a cause. For example it was noted in a study that children in households with lots of books attained higher levels of academic achievement. A potentially incorrect conclusion would be that the presence of books alone causes higher levels of academic achievement when it might just be an indicator of something else that does. Ice cream sales and the incidence of drowning may be correlated, but it is unlikely that the ice cream sales cause the drowning. They may both be related to increased temperatures resulting in more ice cream sales and more people swimming.

A regression analysis on a time series of sales data can be completed quite easily in Excel, using a graph or the FORECAST function.

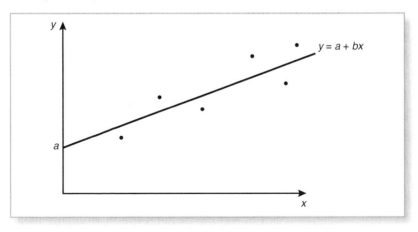

figure 2.1   **The line of best fit**

Example

Month	Period (X)		Sales (Y)
January	1		900
February	2		1,200
March	3		1,500
April (Forecast)	4	Forecast=	

If you are using Excel 2007 or Excel 2010 then enter the above table into Excel, the cell labelled 'Month' goes in cell A1.

- ▪ **Step 1**: chart (graph) the sales data with a scatter graph. Highlight the grey cells and select insert chart, then select 'scatter graph'.

- ▪ **Step 2**: click on the data points on the graph and 'add a trendline'. You have a number of different types of graph you could choose to get the best fit. You also have an option to project the trendline forward by a number of periods with which you can create a forecast.

Excel also contains a function to automatically calculate a linear regression forecast. Type =FORECAST in the cell you want forecast (cell C5) (see the above table). You will then be prompted to enter some cell references for X (this is period 4), known Ys (the known sales for January to March) and known X (periods 1–3). You should end up with FORECAST(B5,C2:C4,B2:B4) in the cell.

Entering the cells and ranges in these functions are confusing. If you enter =FORECAST in cell C5 and click on the *fx* to the left of the box where you enter the cell contents, you will get a pop-up help box to complete the entries for this function.

There are a number of other functions and tools in Excel to help you produce regression analysis and these are described briefly below.

Useful Excel tools

There are a host of tools in Excel to conduct statistical analysis and forecasts. To get to grips with these Excel tools you need to try using them with some real examples. Understanding the tool initially can be confusing and you may need to look at the help functions in Excel. A much better way of gaining a quick insight, getting an introduction to these tools, and more importantly understanding how to use them to their best advantage, is to view one of the hundreds of free tutorials available on **www.youtube.com**.

There are a number of Excel trainers who have created short video tutorials. These trainers have different styles and explanations; you will have your own preferences. The best approach is to view a few tutorials from different trainers and select your favourite. We mention more on this at the end of Chapter 4.

Excel add-ins

There are numerous statistical functions available in Excel through add-ins available as part of Excel 2007 and Excel 2010. Potential additional Excel add-ins are available on the internet.

Some practically useful Microsoft Excel functions for forecasting featured in the Excel Analysis ToolPak to investigate are:

■ regression analysis
■ exponential smoothing
■ moving average.

Forecast frequency and automation

Remember that in most organisations there is a heavy focus on the financial year, although forecasts do not necessarily need to be limited to this particular period. It actually makes more sense to encourage managers to forecast beyond the financial year (see the earlier description of rolling forecasts).

In many organisations, forecasts are completed as part of the budgetary control process. These forecasts may be completed at the end of each quarter or at the end of each month. Forecasts may be produced at the top level by accountants or it may be that forecasts require input from budget managers. If forecasts are going to be produced on a regular basis then it makes sense to automate much of the process and identify the key figures that need to be focused on. In some organisations these regular reforecasts are produced at a high level to give a quick indication to senior managers of likely performance.

If it is already nine months into the year and you are required to produce a budget for the full year, it might be tempting to divide your year-to-date expenditure by nine and multiply by 12. This is not a forecast; this is merely an average extended over the 12 months.

If your sales are rising, the average method would give you an underestimate of your likely forecast sales. If your sales are falling, then the average method would give you an overestimate of your likely forecast sales.

The forecast is supposed to be your prediction of your income and your costs. It may be that some of the calculations of these figures can be internally generated, for example sales forecasts may be generated from details of enquiries and orders.

Run rates may be used to calculate some costs. A run rate is an estimate of the monthly costs for a department or function. Average run rates can be monitored to see if they are rising or falling and then projected forward in the forecast based on this trend rather than an average.

 Remember to put the most effort into forecasting the highly variable, high-impact figures in your forecast. Do not spend a lot of time modelling figures that have little impact or little variability.

Measuring and improving forecast accuracy

The Hackett Group study in 2011[3] of key issues concerning finance directors in major companies concluded that their main concern was the efficiency and effectiveness of the annual budgeting process; the second biggest concern was forecasting performance.

Improving forecasting can have a big impact on improving efficiency and effectiveness. To improve our forecasting we need to start by measuring the accuracy of forecasts. While still remembering that forecasts can never be 100 per cent accurate, we do require them to be 100 per cent useful. Apart from assessing the forecast accuracy with a simple measure, try to develop a qualitative measure of how useful the forecast has been in improving management decisions.

Improving the accuracy of a forecast will also improve forecasting confidence. Consider how much impact a 1 per cent improvement in forecast accuracy would make, or a 1 per cent improvement in your confidence in the forecast on your cash and profit management.

Forecasts are our best estimate of the future. We should not, though, use forecasts as a basis to measure managers' performance. This is

So how do you: incentivise Sales
             : measure performance of Sales?

3 Enterprise Performance Management Research Series, The Hackett Group, 2008–2011.

because by doing so, there will be pressure to produce a forecast that tries to maximise the measure of performance rather than producing a forecast that is based on the best estimate for the future.

Two simple numerical measures of forecast accuracy are:

1 **Mean squared error (MSE)**. The MSE is the average of the square of the 'errors' (the difference between the forecast and actual result) – the lower the MSE figure the better.

2 **Mean absolute percentage error (MAPE)**. The MAPE is the average of percentage 'absolute' differences between the forecast and the actual result:

   – The absolute figures are the differences between actual and forecast – but making all the negative figures positive.
   – These differences are then expressed as a percentage of the 'actual' figure for each period.
   – The percentages for each period are then 'averaged'.

Generally the lower the MAPE the better the forecast.

Example: calculation of MSE and MAPE

Monthly forecast v actual sales (expressed in units)

Period	Forecast	Actual	Error	Error squared	Absolute error	Absolute percentage error
1	100	110	(10)	100.0	10	9.09%
2	110	121	(11)	121.0	11	9.09%
3	121	112	9	81.0	9	8.04%
4	112	115	(3)	9.0	3	2.61%
5	115	116	(1)	1.0	1	0.86%
6	116	118	(2)	4.0	2	1.69%
			Sum	316.0		31.38%
				MSE		**MAPE**
			Average	52.7		5.23%

These measures can be used to compare forecasts produced using different approaches, tools and techniques to give you an idea of which one is most likely to be best. (Generally the lower the MSE or MAPE the more accurate the forecast is.)

The MAPE is widely used, is more intuitive and gives you an impression of the overall forecast accuracy. Both the MSE and the

MAPE have flaws however. Forecasts could be more properly expressed in terms of ranges and confidence levels but many managers find this confusing. Senior managers often want the forecast as a single 'best guess' figure. Perhaps the 'best guess' figure should always be qualified with how we feel about its accuracy and how much the actual figure could deviate from it. A simple alternative is to present a forecast with three figures – best case, best case (with a statement of the probability of hitting it) and worst case (again with a statement of probability). You can generally expect the forecast accuracy to decline the further into the future you forecast.

Using MSE and MAPE

Here are two sales forecasts:

■ Forecast A is based on a three-month (or period) moving average (3PMA).

■ Forecast B is based upon exponential smoothing, with an alpha of 0.7.

The results rounded are shown as follows:

Period	Actual sales	3PMA A	Exponential smoothing B Alpha = 0.7
1	1,160		
2	1,223		1,160
3	1,120		1,204
4	1,150	1,168	1,145
5	1,150	1,164	1,149
6	1,300	1,140	1,150
7	1,400	1,200	1,255
8	1,360	1,283	1,356
9	1,370	1,353	1,359

Note: Forecast values have been rounded.

The MSE and MAPE are calculated for periods 4–9 below:

Period	Absolute error (Rounded)		Error squared			Absolute percentage error	
	A	B	A	B		A	B
4	18	5	312	23		2%	0%
5	14	1	205	2		1%	0%
6	160	150	25,600	22,629		12%	12%
7	200	145	40,000	21,062		14%	10%
8	77	4	5,878	13		6%	0%
9	17	11	278	122		1%	1%
	Average		MSE 12,046	7,309	MAPE	6%	4%

Note: Error values have been rounded. The MSE and MAPE have been calculated with an accurate number.

The MSE and MAPE are lower for the forecast produced using exponential smoothing, so it has been more accurate. Both methods were quite inaccurate for periods 6 and 7 (sales were higher than both forecasts), so it would be worth taking a further look into what happened at this time.

Forecast financial statements

The forecasts may be for sales, profit or cash. Profit and cash forecasts require us to model the income statement (or profit and loss account); the cash flow requires us to model the cash flow statement. We may also want to model the third primary financial statement of the balance sheet – financial statements and modelling them are discussed further in Chapter 3.

New product sales forecasting

New product sales volumes are very difficult to forecast. A frequently used approach is to forecast 'by analogy', taking the sales of similar products and predicting their sales growth following a similar pattern.

New products in many industries tend to have a very high failure rate. Even companies like Apple and Google have launched products that did not take off and were quietly dropped. There are always risks of failure but market research, test marketing and marketing analysis should help to reduce these risks and improve sales forecasts.

Other factors to consider in sales forecasts

When producing sales forecasts it is not possible to inclu
single potential risk and scenario. Other potential factors to
include:

- **short term**: competitor action; supply shortages; commodity prices change
- **longer term**: product life-cycle; competitor action; substitutes; changing technological, economic and social environments; supply shortages.

Below we look at the longer-term factors.

Product life-cycle

All products have a product life-cycle, from birth, hopefully to maturity and inevitably to death. With changing technology many product life-cycles are becoming much shorter. Many organisations need to keep developing their products and launching new ones just to keep them up to date. One of the most extreme examples of this is the mobile phone market; last year's models will not sell today, and consumer and business customers may well delay replacing models until significantly improved products are launched. It is not only product life-cycles that are getting shorter, so too are industry life-cycles. The UK car market took perhaps around 100 years to reach maturity; the mobile phone market took less than 10.

Within our sales forecasting we may need to model the rise and decline of products and maybe even industries as they go through their life-cycles.

Competitor action

Who does Rankin regard as competition? What do clients think?

Competitor campaigns may affect an organisation's sales levels in two ways. They might take sales away from them, but equally they may even stimulate demand for products generally within the industry.

Substitutes

Customers may have a choice of products and services that go beyond traditional competitors. There may be substitutes which they could use instead. For example, in the UK short-haul flights have become cheaper, competing directly with car travel, trains and buses. Likewise, improved video conferencing facilities and services might well reduce the need for business travel.

Need to get a feel for Rankin's place in the market.
Clients - new -v- repeat. If no repeat, why not?

Changing technological, economic and social environments – permanent change

We are living in turbulent times. Many economies around the world received a sudden jolt with the onset of the economic crisis of 2008. Since then, other economic problems have followed, resulting in low economic growth and rising unemployment.

The continual rise of the internet and social networking presents companies with changes in consumer shopping habits and attitudes. For some organisations this is viewed as an opportunity and for others it is a threat. Whatever the impact of these changes, it is certain that in the future forecasting will become more difficult and yet possibly more important. If the future is uncertain then it is more important than ever for organisations to identify opportunities, problems and threats as early as possible. Short-term forecasts may assist with this in explaining what is going on in the marketplace.

Consider the plight of Kodak and how changing technology (or 'disruptive technology') has affected its old market for film and cameras and consequently its business.

Company market capitalisation or value (peak-early 1997)	*US $31,000 million*
Company market value at 5 January 2012	*US $127 million*

As the article overleaf shows, Eastman Kodak, after 131 years of business, filed for Chapter 11 bankruptcy protection on 19 January 2012. Despite being overtaken by technology, Kodak still owns some valuable patents. Some commentators believe these to be worth over US $3 billion. The brand is also very valuable, but the company carries liabilities which bring its overall market value down.

Kodak should have progressed into digital photography much faster. (It could have been first and is credited with building the first digital camera in 1975.) Kodak is thought to have delayed digital photography development as it feared a cannibalisation of its 'cash cow' – conventional film. Such criticisms are of course easy in retrospect. Change hits even the biggest companies and all companies' lives are getting shorter on average. According to Richard Foster from Yale University, since the 1920s the average life span of S & P 500 companies has fallen from 67 years to only 15 years.[4] At what stage is your business?

---

4 Speaking on the BBC News, **www.bbc.co.uk**.

Kodak's inability to evolve led to its demise

By Richard Waters in San Francisco

Eastman Kodak's decision to declare bankruptcy earlier this week is destined to launch a thousand management case studies.

The company that brought photography to a mass market hardly looked like a laggard in the early days of the digital revolution. It invented the digital camera and first distributed pictures on CD-ROM disks two decades ago. If bits and bytes were destined to replace film and photofinishing, the cash cows of its business, then Kodak seemed to know what was needed.

That it ultimately failed to make the transition is testament to the difficulties that industry leaders face in launching into new markets, however aware they may be of the mortal dangers they face.

Kodak has built a handful of inkjet and other digital operations that it hoped would provide the core of a viable business – but that has not been enough to make up for the remorseless erosion of its overall revenues, which have fallen from an annual US $16bn to some US $6bn in the past 20 years.

The cause of its failure, according to the parade of management experts who lined up this week to deliver their verdict: recent generations of Kodak manager were too wedded to the profits from their existing businesses to take radical steps that would have been needed to reposition their company – and its world-leading brand – as a digital leader.

With the breathing-room provided by a Chapter 11 bankruptcy filing, Kodak hopes it will get the chance to restructure and sell off assets to reinvest in its more promising businesses. Whether its creditors will allow it to plough more cash back into its pursuit of a digital future, however, is another matter.

Source: Waters, R. (2012) Kodak's inability to evolve led to its demise, *Financial Times*, 20 January. © The Financial Times Limited 2012. All Rights Reserved.

A major challenge today is to be able to predict potential change and retain the flexibility to react to it quickly. What are the key technological, economic and social changes which are affecting the sales of your organisation's products and services today and what will they be in the future? How will you prepare to cope with the change?

Supply shortages

The global economy is continuing to become more integrated, and therefore more vulnerable to global events. For example, production of cars in Europe may rely on components that have been manufactured in Japan. Following the earthquake in Japan and floods in Thailand in 2011, companies in many industries faced shortages of key components; without these key components production and ultimately sales were constrained.

There were also knock-on effects for other companies supplying into industries that had to limit their production. Supply problems do not need to be caused by something as dramatic and unpredictable as the natural disasters of 2011 – strikes, machine breakdowns and corporate failures are more likely. Planning and therefore budgeting should take account of these risks.

Exercise

1 At what stage in their lives are your organisation's products?

2 What are the 'disruptive technologies' (and other changes) in your industry?

3 How do you monitor them?

4 Does your product or service have any potential substitutes? (Substitutes are alternative products or services which could meet the customers' needs.)

5 How does your business monitor competitor action?

6 How have competitor actions affected your organisation's sales over the past 12 months?

7 What are the main potential substitutes for your organisation's products and services?

8 Has your organisation ever been faced with shortages in the supply of key components or materials?

9 What are the risks of shortages in the future?

10 How could you better manage them?

3

Essential background financial skills for budgeting

What is the relationship between Cost, Value, Cash and Risk? How do we account for income and costs? How does this differ from cash flow? What do I need to understand about costs and cost behaviour? These questions are addressed in this chapter.

Cheaper is not always better: cost and value in budgeting

Oscar Wilde said: 'A cynic is a man who knows the price of everything and the value of nothing.' To build and manage budgets you need to know (or understand) the cost and value of everything.

When we make our own purchasing decisions for a personal expenditure, whether we are purchasing clothes, food or entertainment, we usually base them on both cost and value.

Some of our purchases we might consider to be commodities where our selection can be made solely on the basis of cost – cheapest is best. For example, when buying petrol we might seek out the cheapest petrol station to make a purchase, but in practice most of us buy petrol from a station which is convenient and is on our journey and we do not want to waste time looking for the cheapest. People and companies may have a different idea of values. Some clothes customers are satisfied with cheap unbranded products, others prefer more expensive designer labels.

Similarly, when we make our purchases with our budgets at work, we should not make our decisions purely based on the costs as there may be factors that mean the cheapest is not the best. Our purchase should not be based on the cheapest option, but the 'best value for money' option: the option that gives us the most for our money. To define what good 'value for money' is we not only need to know the costs, we also need to be able to make a judgement about the value of what we are purchasing. We should make our choices based on what meets our needs most cost effectively.

We may make savings in staff costs by employing fewer staff or recruiting less skilled or less experienced staff on lower rates of pay. This may affect an important aspect of customer service and our savings may be counterbalanced by reduced sales. When managers are given a budget they have to make their judgements based on the costs and the consequences of making savings or spending more.

Exercise

Take a few minutes to think about a purchasing or cost saving decision from your own organisation where money was saved at the expense of customer service or something similar (you can include internal customers in your consideration).

When we are making cost savings we have to start with what is important, what must be preserved and what can be discarded. Your judgements should consider both cost and value. To be a good budget manager you need to understand the cost of everything *and* the value of everything.

Accruals, cash and commitment accounting and budgeting

This section covers financial statements and accounting principles. If you are already expert in this area you could skip through it, though you may still find the material useful for coaching your team or other colleagues. If you are not an expert you will benefit from working through the exercises and examples. You should also feel comfortable about asking for explanations from your finance colleagues – they are there to help and support you.

When we work with small businesses we often find owners and directors confused by financial statements produced by their external firms of accountants. If your accountants are not producing reports and information that are useful to you they are not doing their job. Taking the accounting 'in-house' will probably help some business owners improve their understanding.

Non-accountants often get confused between the differences in cash, profits ('accrual based') and commitments. In most organisations the accounts are produced on an accruals basis. This means that income is recorded as it is earned; this is when we supply goods and services. Costs are recorded when we receive the benefits from those costs (this concept is explained further with examples later in this chapter).

When we order goods and services we may well record these in our accounts as a commitment. If you do not have a sophisticated finance system you could just record these in a spreadsheet or an accounts book. Monitoring your commitments (rather than just your expenditure) and what you have left to make decisions over can be a useful approach to staying within a budget. If you do this, try to think about expenditure which might not be recorded as a commitment yet is effectively committed, such as future staff pay and contracted services.

Profit is a measure of performance and in many organisations it is the only measure of performance. Profit is the amount which has been earned less resources consumed over a period. Profits are accounted for on an accruals basis; this means there will be a difference between the budget for profit and the budget for cash. It also means that a business can be profitable and run out of cash (or go bankrupt) and yet a loss-making business can still generate cash and stay in business.

Costs

Example 1

Rex Retail Limited operates a number of shops across the country. Each shop has a manager with full budget responsibility. Every month the managers review their branch profit and loss account (known as the P&L). The rental charge is always the same every month even though rent is paid every quarter. If rent is accounted for when it is paid quarterly, then the shop would appear to be performing badly in those months and well in the other months. To give a better picture of performance the rent should be charged to the period that it belongs to.

The same principle will apply to rates and insurance premiums. These costs are being accounted for on an accruals basis rather than a cash basis. Small costs may simply be accounted for when they are invoiced.

If your company uses a comprehensive accounting system such as SAP R4 or Oracle you may find costs are accounted for when you take receipt of goods and services.

Exercise

Review your own budgets – which costs are spread out over a period and which are accounted for when invoiced? Or does this happen when the goods or services are received from the supplier?

Capital costs: the difference between capital expenditure and revenue expenditure

Example 2

Rex Retail refits each of its shops every five years at a cost of £100,000. This cost is not charged directly to the P&L account as it is a capital cost, or capital expenditure.

Capital expenditure is capitalised – i.e. treated as a fixed asset and written off over its useful life (in this case five years). Each branch will see this refit cost as an annual depreciation charge of £20,000. (£100,000 divided between five years). Revenue expenditure costs are charged directly to the branches' P&L account. (Further explanation and examples of capital expenditure, depreciation and their impact on the financial statements are given later in this chapter.)

Exercise

Take a moment to review your budget.

1 Do you have any depreciation charges? (These would relate to fixed assets that are used by your business unit or department.)

2 Do you have a capital budget? (This would be a budget for spending on plant and equipment.)

Income

Revenue is recorded in the P&L account when it is earned. In the case of a retailer, the sale and receipt of cash is normally the same. Most companies give credit to their customers, so income will be earned at a different time from when cash is received from customers. In some businesses where customers pay in advance, income will still not be recognised until the goods or services have been delivered. It is important to understand the difference between income and receipts when budgeting for profit and cash flow.

Example

Question

Titan Training was commissioned to deliver an in-house training course. It received the order in January, delivered the programme in February, raised its invoice to the client in March and finally received payment in April. In which month did Titan Training earn its fee?

Answer

The fee was earned in February when the training was delivered; it is recorded as income for February.

Question

Titan Training also runs public programmes and customers normally pay in advance for these programmes. Titan ran a programme in May. The delegates paid the company in April. When should Titan recognise the income for the training course?

Answer

The income should be recognised in May when the service was delivered.

Understanding profit and loss account figures

Income

If you have income in your budgets have you ever had a problem reconciling the figures? Income in the P&L account should be recognised when it is earned. This is generally when the goods and services a company supplies are delivered. There may be some seasonality in your income; this seasonality should also be reflected in your original budget otherwise you will find variances that are purely caused by poor phasing of the original budget. When you put together your budget you need to understand when the income is likely to arise.

Expenditure or costs

You need to understand your expenditure or costs and how they are accounted for. Costs should be accounted for in the period when you gain the benefit, rather than when you pay for them.

Understanding the difference between profits (accounted for on what is called an accruals basis) and cash is fundamental when you are producing budgets.

Example

For example, the cost of a quarterly rent bill should be spread out across the months it relates to. The budget should be put together on the same basis, with $\frac{1}{12}$ of the annual rent being budgeted each month, and the cost of the rent being allocated to each month on the same basis. Even though rent is being charged into each month's P&L account, it will still actually be paid each quarter and this will affect the cash flow.

Tip: understanding accrual accounting

You may come across the terms accruals, accruing or accrued. Whenever you encounter them it is more helpful to substitute the word 'matching'. Accruals accounting is just about matching costs to periods.

At the end of each period we may have to calculate accruals – costs that have arisen but may not have been invoiced by our supplier. To charge them to the period we need to 'accrue' the cost and further details are given below.

Review of accruals accounting

1 A timing difference

Profit and cash are different in the short run; in the very long run they should be the same. The timing of profit can be quite different from the timing of cash flow, as profit is accounted for on an accruals basis.

Income may be earned at a different time from when it is paid. There may be sales that have not been paid, i.e. there are outstanding debtors, or there may be goods and services that have been used but not paid for. In some companies, such as tour operators, customers pay in advance.

Costs hit the profit and loss account at a different time from when they are paid. A company may have purchased stock or inventory, the cost of which does not hit the P&L account when it is bought, but later on when benefits are gained from it. Both debtors and stock are part of the working capital (summarised below). Accounting for income and expenditure on an accrual accounting basis also requires us to account for assets and liabilities in the balance sheet (described in more detail later in this chapter), including working capital, fixed assets and funding.

2 Working capital

Working capital is made up of debtors (accounts receivable), stock (inventory) and creditors (accounts payable).

Debtors are customers to whom we have sold goods or service and who have not yet paid. Sales appear in the P&L accounts as income but do not appear in the cash flow statement. When the customer pays it will be recorded in the cash flow.

Our creditors are the organisations we owe money to and for most of us our main creditors will be our suppliers.

Stock or inventory is made up of raw materials, work in progress (part finished goods) and finished goods, or goods for resale. Stock is generally valued at the lower of cost or net realisable value (the value stock can be sold for, less the costs to sell it).

There is more detailed coverage of budgeting and managing working capital in Chapter 5.

3 Fixed assets, capital expenditure and depreciation

A depreciation charge for capital items is charged in the P&L account but does not affect the company's cash flow. Cash flow is affected by the purchase of fixed assets, such as plant, machinery and equipment, and fixed assets are also known as 'non-current assets'. Fixed assets are assets that give a long-term benefit to the organisation. They are written off (or charged against profit) over this period. There are several ways of sharing the depreciation costs to years; the most commonly used method is the 'straight line method'.

Example: accounting for depreciation and fixed assets

Assume a company purchased a van for £25,000 cash. It plans to use the van for three years then sell it for £7,000 cash. Over the three years the van will have decreased in value by £18,000. The annual depreciation would be £6,000 per year (on a 'straight line' basis). This would be £6,000 charged to the P&L account (or income statement) each year. Depreciation would not affect the cash flow. The cash would be reduced by £25,000 when the van was bought; it would increase by £7,000 at the end of year 3 when the van was sold.

The van would show in the balance sheet as £25,000 at the beginning of year 1 and at the end of year 1 its net book value (NBV) would be shown as £25,000 – £6,000 = £19,000, which may bear little relationship to the market value of the van. At the end of year 2 the balance sheet NBV would fall to £19,000 – £6,000 = £13,000, and finally in year 3 it would fall to £13,000 – £6,000 = £7,000. If the van is sold for more than the book value this would result in a 'profit on disposal of fixed asset'; if it sells for less this would be a 'loss on disposal of fixed asset'.

4 Funding

There are two means of funding a business – using the owners' or shareholders' money (equity) or borrowing money (loan capital). New loans or loan repayments do not affect the company's profit other than the impact of the resultant interest charges. Similarly if the company issues new shares to raise more capital there is no impact on profit. Many businesses increase their capital most years by reinvesting some of the profits.

Direct and indirect methods of producing cash flow statements

There are two ways of producing a cash flow. The simplest method is to list out all of your receipts and payments using an approach called the 'direct approach'.

The cash flows within published accounts are normally produced using the indirect approach. The indirect approach starts the cash flow with the figure for profit and then reconciles the differences between profit and cash. The indirect method is a much better method of highlighting where cash has gone and where it has come from.

When a budget is put together, you are normally putting together budgets for profit and for loss. You might also produce budgets for cash flow. Cash flow budgets can be prepared using the direct method or the indirect method, but the latter method is normally easier. In order to budget cash using the indirect method you need to forecast the depreciation, changes in working capital, investment and funding.

Worked examples of direct and indirect cash flows are given later in this chapter but the basic formats are as shown in Table 3.1.

table 3.1   Cash flow for the year: basic formats

Direct cash flow

Add receipts (cash in)	XXX
Less payments (cash out)	(XXX)
Cash flow for period	XXX

Indirect cash flow

Operating profit	XXX
Add back depreciation	XXX
Changes in working capital*	
Stock (inventory)	XXX
Debtors (accounts receivable)	XXX
Creditors	XXX
Less tax paid	(XXX)
Less interest paid (plus interest received)	(XXX)
Investing (e.g. purchase of new assets)	(XXX)
Financing (e.g. new loans, new shares)	XXX
Cash flow for the year	XXX

Note: increase in stock reduces cash, reduction in stock increases cash; increase in debtors reduces cash, reduction in debtors increases cash; reduction in creditors reduces cash, increase in creditors increases cash.

The balance sheet

The three primary financial statements within a business are the profit and loss (P&L) account (or income statement), the cash flow and the balance sheet.

For most non-accountants, the balance sheet is a complete mystery. It is merely a list of assets and liabilities on a given day and is often described as a snapshot of the business. It is called a balance sheet because it is simply a list of balances. If you go into your accounting system on any given day and take the balances on each account within the system you could produce a balance sheet. As described earlier, many of the changes in the balances over a period will represent the differences between profit and cash. You will see this by working through the examples of the financial statements given in the following pages.

The balance sheet is probably the least useful of the financial statements. It is possible to produce some budgets without understanding the balance sheet. If you are producing an organisation-wide budget, perhaps for a small business, you may also need to produce a budgeted balance sheet.

In the balance sheet, the assets of the business are classified as either fixed assets (or non-current assets) and current assets.

Fixed assets are the long-term assets of the business, and they include:

■ tangible assets such as plant, machinery and equipment
■ long-term investments
■ intangible assets (such as brand names, patents and goodwill).

Current assets are short-term assets, and they include:

■ stock (or inventory)
■ debtors (or accounts receivable)
■ cash.

The liabilities of the business are also classified as being non-current (long-term liabilities that are due in more than 12 months) and current (liabilities that are due within 12 months). The main type of non-current liability will typically be long-term bank loans. The main type of current liability is trade creditors (or accounts payable).

The sum of all the assets less the sum of all the liabilities equals the net assets. The net assets balance with the 'shareholders' funds'. You can think about the shareholders' funds as being the amount owed to the shareholders by the company or what the shareholders have invested in the company. The 'net assets' figure does not tell you the value of the business; the value of a budget is more likely to be related to future potential profit. There are alternative balance sheet layouts and these are illustrated in Figure 3.1. They represent the 'balance sheet equation':

Net assets = shareholders' funds

Fixed assets + current assets – current liabilities – long-term liabilities
= shareholders' funds

or

Fixed assets + current assets
= shareholders' funds + long-term liabilities + current liabilities

or

Fixed assets + current assets – current liabilities
= shareholders' funds + long-term liabilities

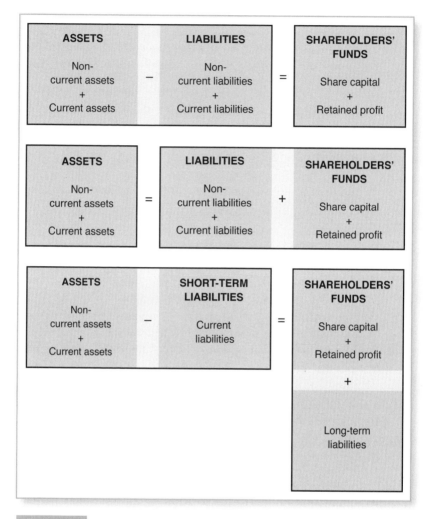

figure 3.1   **Alternative balance sheet layouts**

Simple model of the financial statements

Figure 3.2 shows the relationship between the financial statements. Changes in profit, cash, working capital, fixed assets and funding will change the year's balance sheet. Cash and profit are different, but profit affects cash flow – the long-run cash and profit are the same. Cash will also be changed by movements in working capital, the sale or purchase of fixed assets and changes in funding. Depreciation reduces profit and fixed asset values but does not affect cash.

Simple illustration of the financial statements

This is a simplified model for a trading business that buys and sells goods. It is designed to help you to understand the financial statements and how they fit together. The example also shows you the difference between the direct and indirect methods of producing the cash flow statements. To make the example simpler there are no dividends for shareholders and no taxation.

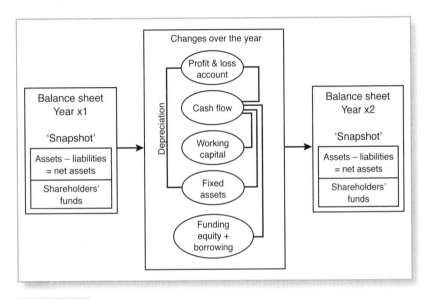

figure 3.2   The relationship between the financial statements

Exercise

1 Try to work through the income statements, cash flows and balance sheets to see if you can see where the figures have come from and how the statements interrelate.

2 Review the published statements of your own organisation to see how the model matches them.

3 If you have access to internal management reports try the same exercise using those.

4 As an extra learning challenge you could create a spreadsheet model of the financial statement from the example, then using this model make an estimate (or forecast) for year 4's financial

statements. Which way do you think they are heading for the year's profit and the closing cash balance? (Note: forecasting the profit requires you to forecast income and costs. Forecasting the cash also primarily requires you to forecast the working capital (inventory, accounts receivable and accounts payable) in addition to profit. (Modelling and managing working capital is covered in more detail in Chapter 5.) Forecasting cash using the 'indirect' cash flow method should be easiest. Forecasting the balance sheet will give you the least benefit out of the three financial statements.)

Income statement (P&L account)

	Year 1 £000s	Year 2 £000s	Year 3 £000s
Sales	1000	1200	1300
Less cost of sales	(500)	(610)	(670)
Gross profit	500	590	630
Gross margin (gross profit/sales)	50%	49%	48%
Less operating expenses	(400)	(500)	(600)
Operating profit	100	90	30
Operating profit margin (operating profit/sales)	10%	8%	2%
Less interest (on borrowings)	(10)	(11)	(11)
Profit after interest	90	79	19

Balance sheet movements – working capital

	Year 1 £000s	Year 2 £000s	Year 3 £000s
1. Inventory (stock)			
Opening (balance at start of period)	30	60	90
Purchases	530	640	670
Sold	(500)	(610)	(670)
Closing (balance at end of period)	60	90	90
2. Accounts receivable (debtors) – customers			
Opening (balance at start of period)	110	210	310
Add credit sales	1000	1200	1300

Less payments by customers	(900)	(1100)	(1200)
Closing (balance at end of period)	210	310	410

3. Accounts payable (creditors) – suppliers

Opening (balance at start of period)	60	80	200
Add credit purchases	530	640	670
Less payments to suppliers	(510)	(520)	(620)
Closing (balance at end of period)	80	200	250

Balance sheet movements – non-current assets (fixed assets)

Opening (balance at start of period)	100	110	150
Add new assets purchased	50	100	50
Less assets sold	0	0	0
Less assets depreciation over period	(40)	(60)	(60)
Closing (balance at end of period)	110	150	140

Balance sheet movements – borrowing

Opening borrowing	100	100	110
Add new borrowing	0	10	0
Less repayments	0	0	0
Closing balance	100	110	110

Cash flow – indirect method

	Year 1 £000s	Year 2 £000s	Year 3 £000s
Operating profit	100	90	30
Add back depreciation	40	60	60
	140	150	90
Change in working capital			
Inventory	(30)	(30)	0
Accounts receivable	(100)	(100)	(100)
Accounts payable	20	120	50
	(110)	(10)	(50)
Interest paid	(10)	(11)	(11)
Cash flow from operating activities	20	129	29

Cash flow from investing activities	"		"
Capital expenditure – new non-current assets	(50)	(100)	(50)
Cash flow from financing activities	"		"
New loans	0	10	0
Change in cash	(30)	39	(21)
Cash opening balance	40	10	49
Change in cash	(30)	39	(21)
Closing balance	10	49	28

Cash flow – direct method

	Year 1 £000s	Year 2 £000s	Year 3 £000s
Cash in			
Cash receipts from customers	900	1100	1200
New loans	0	10	0
	900	1110	1200
Cash out			
Cash payment to suppliers	(510)	(520)	(620)
Cash expenses (operating expenses less depreciation)	(360)	(440)	(540)
Purchase of fixed assets	(50)	(100)	(50)
Interest	(10)	(11)	(11)
Loan repayments	0	0	0
	(930)	(1071)	(1221)
Cash change over period	(30)	39	(21)

Balance sheet as at year end

	Year 1 £000s	Year 2 £000s	Year 3 £000s
Non-current assets (fixed assets)	110	150	140
Current assets			
Inventory (stock)	60	90	90
Accounts receivable (debtors)	210	310	410
Cash	10	49	28
	280	449	528

Current liabilities
   (short term due in the next 12 months)

Accounts payable (creditors)	(80)	(200)	(250)
Non-current liabilities (long-term) – loans	(100)	(110)	(110)
Net assets	**210**	**289**	**308**
Share capital	100	100	100
Retained profit at start of year	20	110	189
Retained profit for the year	90	79	19
Shareholders' funds	**210**	**289**	**308**

The master budget

The master budget is the comprehensive budget for the organisation. It includes a budgeted income statement, a balance sheet and a cash flow statement. To produce the master budget you need an understanding of accruals accounting and how the three financial statements fit together. If you are producing the budget for your department, it will ultimately need to fit into the overall master budget.

Components of the master budget for a manufacturing business could be:

- sales budget
- production budget
- material budgeting/direct materials budget
- labour budget
- manufacturing overhead budget
- ending finished goods inventory budget
- cash budget
- selling and administrative expense budget
- budgeted income statement
- budgeted balance sheet.

There are a number of potential starting points to the budget, depending upon the circumstances of the company. Forecast sales, production capacity, cash and required profit are normally the major issues – these are a combination of objectives and limiting factors. A consumer goods company may start with a sales forecast, leading to planning production to meet the expected demand. A commodity bulk chemicals company may start with its production capacity, planning to run at full production to minimise its production costs. This company will probably be a 'price taker' – taking the market price to sell their capacity.

In the years before the downturn of 2008, many UK companies were driven to set a budget to achieve a profit target. This budget was usually based on beating the previous year's profit performance – normally by selling more. In the years that have followed the downturn, many firms have had to change their focus to trying to hold on to their existing profits – often by cost cutting. For many companies bank borrowing has become more difficult and some companies have had to change their priority from making profits to generating cash in order to become self-funding or pay back loans.

Exercise

What do you think the starting point is for the budget in your organisation? What is your current priority: growth, sales, survival, profit or cash?

Within all organisations budgets need to be co-ordinated. This may be done through a small team of senior managers often known as a budget committee.

Costs

Choice of cost headings

Budgeting is often influenced or even driven by account headings or titles. Breaking down costs into too much detail may create extra work without producing useful information, but insufficient detail makes analysis difficult. Ideally your account breakdown should help you analyse why you are incurring costs rather than just a description of the costs. For example consider the benefit of describing spending money on an advertising leaflet as promotion rather than just printing.

Exercise

Take a few moments to review the account headings and descriptions in your management reports. Could they be improved to make budgeting or analysis better?

Costs and cost structure

When budgeting for costs, we need to understand what drives costs. Normally we think of costs as being either fixed or variable. Fixed costs are costs which are fixed irrespective of volume. For example, the rent on a shop may be considered fixed as no matter what the shop sells, the rent will be the same. Whereas the cost of the merchandise it sells, or maybe the bags and wrappings for customers will be variable costs: therefore as sales increase these costs increase too.

When we build a budget we are really building a model of our business and the relationship between volume and costs. Some costs will be stepped, so once certain volumes are reached, the costs jump upwards. For example, staff costs would normally be considered fixed costs in a shop. However, at some busy times with increasing customers and sales, the shop may need to take on extra staff, so the costs step up with volume.

There are other factors that drive costs other than the volume of sales. Activity based costing (ABC) is an approach that tries to understand and model some of these other cost drivers.

Activity based costing is often said to be costing for complexity. If we increase complexity we increase activity and this increases costs. This sophisticated approach to costing has been taken up by very few firms, probably because as an approach it is very complex. Despite this, firms can still borrow some of the ideas from ABC. The idea is that the way to decrease costs is to decrease complexity and variety. More standardisation leads to lower costs. Further details about ABC are covered later in this chapter.

When you are trying to build a model of your costs, try to think about the factors that influence them and then drive most of your efforts into understanding the big costs. A small cost can be roughly estimated without too much loss.

Fixed and variable costs

Example: the baker's shop

Consider a baker's shop. The rent and rates of the shop are the same no matter how many cakes the bakery bakes and sells within a week. If it increases its sales and baking it consumes more ingredients, which are the variable costs. There is a direct relationship between the amount of products produced and the cost of producing them.

Textbooks often define costs as being clearly fixed or clearly variable, but this is an oversimplification. In the short term, many of our costs may be more fixed. The bakery shop may be committed to production without any guarantee that the cakes will sell. In the long term, costs which might be considered fixed may be variable. For example, if sales from the shop increase then the shop may need to take on an extra worker. If the sales fall, the shop may reduce its staff. If the sales fall enough, the business owner may be better off closing the shop and saving the rent.

Managers often misunderstand the term variable costs. For example, the cost of heating and lighting may vary throughout the year because of changes in the weather. These costs, however, are unlikely to vary with the volume of products produced and sold, and so these costs would be described as fixed. Variable costs are more likely to be easily traced back to the product or service and are more likely to be 'direct costs'.

When managers focus on managing costs they often consider fixed costs to be costs which cannot be altered. This is not necessarily true. Just because costs are called fixed does not mean that savings cannot be made.

When making savings in any cost, whether it is fixed or variable, we must ensure the savings are made without damaging the quality of the product or service. Quality is in the 'eyes of the customer'. Cutting the amount of cream in a cream cake might save money but might destroy its value to the customer – switching to a cheaper dairy supplier might cut cost without compromising customer value.

Value analysis and value engineering

Value analysis and engineering were techniques developed during the Second World War by the major US company General Electric. Shortages of resources forced General Electric to look for substitutes for both labour and materials. In doing this, they discovered potential cost savings which were delivered without any compromise to the performance of the finished product.

The main principle behind value analysis and value engineering is to reduce cost without affecting the value to the end customer, or without affecting the functioning of the product for whatever it was designed for.

A good starting point is to define precisely what customer requirements are and what the product is delivering for the customer. In some instances rather than trying to cut costs, companies have found they can actually add slightly more cost to add a lot more extra value, which can then be charged for back to the customer.

In the UK, the main premium supermarket is Marks & Spencer. Marks & Spencer sells premium groceries at a premium price. When you purchase a Marks & Spencer's cake you know it will be good! Customers are prepared to pay a little more to get this expected and assured quality. By spending a little more on the product ingredients, the packaging and the production of the cake the company may be delivering a lot more extra added value.

In contrast, discount supermarkets compete predominantly on price, their priority being to cut costs where they can. If they made their products 'better' and charged slightly more the improved quality would not necessarily be appreciated by their customers who are focused more on the product cost.

We can think of the price the customer is prepared to pay for a product or service as what the customer values that product or service as being. Ultimately all businesses make profit by delivering more value to customers. It may be necessary for the business to incur some extra cost to deliver this extra value.

Exercise

Successful businesses recognise where they can most effectively add value. Do you know how your business adds value most effectively?

There may be some functions performed by a business which add very little value and may be better contracted out. Apple adds the most value in its design and marketing. All of the assembly of Apple products is contracted out (at the moment much of it to a company in China called Foxconn). The assembly of electronic products is a low value-adding activity. Apple focuses its attention where it adds the most value – design and marketing.

Organisations and their budget managers need to understand the relationship between costs and value. To slightly misquote Oscar Wilde, accountants sometimes know 'the cost of everything and the value of nothing'. Budget managers need to understand both the cost and value of everything.

Quote

Charles Haskell Revson (1906–1975) founder of the Revlon cosmetics company said: 'In the factory we make cosmetics; in the store we sell hope.' Revson's factory manufactured cosmetics, but the benefit, or the real value that its products would be delivering was something rather more intangible: he jokingly described it as hope.

You need to work out where costs can be saved without affecting the performance of your department in terms of delivering what your customers are looking for.

Example

In recent years budget airlines have been very successful. Often they follow a model developed by Southwest Airlines in the US. Budget airlines like Southwest Airlines, easyJet and Ryanair are often referred to as 'no-frills' airlines. They have cut the frills that do not add value.

If you are seeking convenient transportation for a short hop you probably are not interested in a free in-flight meal and in-flight entertainment. Essentially these customers are looking for a bus in the sky. The most important aspects of booking a flight then becomes the cost and reliability rather than the old-fashioned glitz and glamour of airline travel.

Some travellers still prefer the old-fashioned standards and shun the budget airlines but budget airlines are not trying to reach these customers. Southwest Airlines is now the largest domestic carrier in the US, while several of the other traditional airlines struggle with bankruptcy.

Value analysis in 'not-for-profit' organisations

The same principles can also be applied within not-for-profit organisations such as charities or public sector organisations.

When looking at making savings we should consider how the savings affect us achieving the objectives of the organisation. This may be especially difficult within charity and public service organisations which may have multiple objectives and multiple demands competing for their (often very limited) resources.

Public sector organisations should look at how they deliver value to their stakeholders; these will include service users, taxpayers and the state. Similarly, charities have to review whether they are delivering value to their stakeholders. These stakeholders will principally be the charity's beneficiaries but could also include donors and funders.

The concepts of value are applied within a public sector model called 'value for money' or the VFM model. Further details of the VFM approach are covered in Chapter 7. This model can be adapted for use in all not-for-profit organisations. It is also a model which could be used within a cost centre in a commercial business.

Exercise

1 Who are your organisation's customers and what is it about your product or service that is most valuable to them?

2 How might your organisation best cut costs without destroying customer value?

3 Where does your organisation and department add value most effectively?

Relevant costs for budgeting

To manage costs effectively, managers need to understand how costs behave and which costs change with different decisions.

We have already considered costs as being either fixed or variable. Costs can either be fixed with volume or be variable (going up with volume). There could be other 'cost drivers' too, or other factors that affect costs. Activity based costing is an approach that tries to model some of these other factors.

Overhead cost recovery: how overheads are charged back to products and services

Costs can be described as being either direct or indirect (also called overheads). Direct costs are those costs that are directly attributable to a product or service and are normally direct labour or direct materials. They could also be direct expenses. The terminology originates from the manufacturing industry and is difficult to translate into many service businesses. The word 'overhead' is generally thought of in negative terms, but it may be that the overhead is the extra cost that adds the important extra value.

Think about the manufacture of a table. The wood, metal and plastic that go directly into the making of the table are the *direct materials*. The labour is the people who make the table and is considered *direct labour*. Then assume that the table is manufactured in a factory along with several other products. The factory has a monthly rental charge and this monthly rental charge may be considered an *indirect cost* or *overhead*. This is because it does not belong to a single product, but to the total manufacturing capability of the factory.

It might be considered beneficial to attribute the indirect costs back to individual products so that the profitability of individual products can be established. If all of the products are much the same it would be reasonable to divide the overhead by the number of products manufactured within a period to gain a rate per unit. If the factory manufactures a range of differing products, it may not be reasonable to charge the overhead on this basis. Overheads are normally charged in proportion to labour content.

Now assume that the factory manufactures tables and chairs, and that a table takes three direct labour hours to make and a chair takes one and a half direct labour hours to make. In this situation it might seem reasonable to charge twice as much overhead to a table than to a chair. This is not necessarily so because direct labour is just one basis of charging or recovering overheads.

Rather than using direct labour hours it would be possible to share the cost out between the products based on machine time. Perhaps to manufacture a table only takes one machine hour whereas the manufacture of a chair may take one and a half machine hours. In this instance the chair may take a bigger proportion of the overhead.

This type of overhead recovery or *overhead absorption* was developed over 100 years ago when manufacturing industry was very different from today. Maybe it was reasonable to assume that most of the overhead was in some way related to labour content or machine content.

For many businesses today, overheads as a proportion of the total cost have increased. It is now becoming more important to focus not just on controlling and managing the direct costs but also the indirect costs or overheads.

Some companies choose not to try to recover overheads in their product costings, and this approach is known as *marginal costing* or *direct costing*. There is a potential problem that without attempting to include overheads within our product costings, we may well be tempted to under-recover costs within pricing.

Activity based costing (ABC)

In some organisations, overheads have been growing and now may well be bigger than direct costs. With this change in organisations' costs has come activity based costing (ABC). The approach was developed by Professor Robert Kaplan at Harvard Business School in the 1980s.

Under ABC the focus is no longer on costing the product but costing the processes. The costs of the processes are charged back to products and services according to how they use that process or activity.

Activity based costing has been heavily promoted by both academics and consultants in the past. Most businesses though have chosen to avoid this technique, believing the approach to be too complicated. The method also still requires assumptions and allocations of cost just like absorption costing.

Even if you do not or never will operate ABC you can still use some of the ideas from the theory. One idea from ABC is that managers do not manage costs, instead they manage activity. To reduce our costs we need to either reduce our activity or find a simpler way of performing the activity. The main opportunities to reduce needless activity are to reduce needless complexity and variety (needless complexity and variety would be complexity and variety which adds no value to customers). This includes:

- Reducing or standardising products and services and components (example savings – inventory storage and holding, less time switching resources between different products and services, more efficient production/operations).
- Reducing the number of suppliers (example savings – fewer purchase orders and supplier relationships to manage).
- Reducing the number of customers (example savings – fewer customer relationships and accounts to manage – smaller customers rather than being dropped may be served more economically through agents or a different service).
- Reducing cost centres and business units (example savings – reduced administration and accounting).
- Reducing sites (example savings – reduced property costs and travel between sites).

Example

Consider a business that manufactures 100 products with each product using 100 components. How much complexity is there within its production? How much does this complexity cost the business in extra overheads?

If the company works to rationalise its product range to just 20 products and the components to just 20 standard components we can see there will be a massive reduction in the complexity of manufacturing, probably resulting in an overall reduction in cost.

Apart from rationalising the product range and the products' components, companies can also reduce complexity and variety by reducing the number of suppliers and the number of customers. It may sound like a strange idea to try to find improvements by reducing the number of customers, but sometimes it is the case that some smaller customers may well cost more to serve than they deliver in extra profit.

A benefit of ABC is that it can be used not only to cost products but also to cost customers and produce a customer profitability analysis, which reviews the profitability by customer after allocating a proportion of the indirect costs to each account. Perhaps your organisation may have some customers who cost you more to serve than they give you in gross profit?

Exercise

1 List out the opportunities to reduce complexity and variety in your department or organisation (without reducing value).

2 For each opportunity describe which costs are likely to be reduced by this simplification.

3 Try to make an estimate of what the savings might be.

The breakeven model

One of the simplest financial models is called a breakeven model. With the breakeven model we can work out what volumes of sales are needed to cover costs and therefore to break even. The model is fundamentally about the company's cost structure, its mix between costs that are fixed with volume and costs that are variable with volume.

Example

Remember the cake shop with monthly fixed costs of rent, rates, heat, light, insurance and staff. These fixed costs amount to £10,000 each month. The shop makes and sells cakes. The cakes retail for £1.00 each and they have ingredient costs of £0.20. When each cake is sold it makes a contribution of £0.80 (contribution is sales less variable costs). How many cakes does the shop need to sell in order to break even?

The breakeven calculation is a simple division of the total fixed costs for the month by the unit contribution made on each cake. £10,000 divided by a unit contribution of £0.80 gives a breakeven of 12,500 cakes (see Table 3.2). Breakeven can also be expressed in terms of sales revenue. To work out the breakeven point in terms of sales revenue, simply divide the fixed costs by the contribution rate. The contribution rate is the contribution (sales minus variable costs) divided by the revenue.

In the cake shop example, the contribution rate is 80 per cent. In other words, for all sales 80 per cent of sales turn into extra contribution and ultimately extra profit. The fixed costs are £10,000 for the month. This figure divided by the contribution rate of 80 per cent gives a breakeven at sales of £12,500. The breakeven model can be illustrated in a graph (see Figure 3.5).

The breakeven graph is a graph of sales revenue against volume superimposed over a graph of costs against volume. The fixed costs is a horizontal line, the variable cost line slopes upwards with increasing volume. Where the total costs line and the sales line cross is the breakeven point.

table 3.2   **Cake shop breakeven figures**

Cakes sold	Sales	Fixed costs	£ Variable costs	Total costs	Profit	
0	0	10,000	0	10,000	(10,000)	
2,500	2,500	10,000	500	10,500	(8,000)	
5,000	5,000	10,000	1,000	11,000	(6,000)	
7,500	7,500	10,000	1,500	11,500	(4,000)	
10,000	10,000	10,000	2,000	12,000	(2,000)	
12,500	**12,500**	**10,000**	**2,500**	**12,500**	0	*Breakeven*
15,000	15,000	10,000	3,000	13,000	2,000	
17,500	17,500	10,000	3,500	13,500	4,000	
20,000	20,000	10,000	4,000	14,000	6,000	

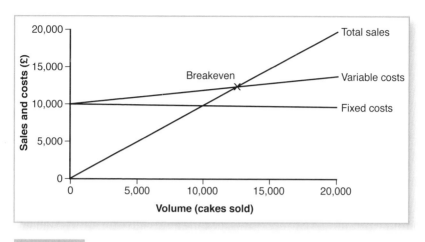

figure 3.3   Breakeven for a cake shop

Cost structure

The cost structure of a company relates to how many of its costs are fixed and how many of them are variable. Understanding the organisation's cost structure is important in determining what has the biggest impact on the organisation's financial performance. This will have a big effect on our approach to budgets and budgeting. It is important to fully understand your organisation's cost structure to know where your main effort should be directed when building the budget and managing it.

Example

There are two companies, A and B:

■ **Company A** – most of its costs are variable costs; it has a low rate of contribution.

■ **Company B** – most of its costs are fixed costs; it has a high rate of contribution. Extra sales turn into a lot of extra contribution.

The profit and loss accounts for the two companies are given below. Both companies have the same initial sales and the same initial profit. The tables also show the impact of a 25 per cent increase in sales and a 25 per cent reduction in sales.

Company A (£)

		Sales increase 25%	Sales decrease 25%
Sales	100,000	125,000	75,000
Less variable costs	(80,000)	(100,000)	(60,000)
Contribution	20,000	25,000	15,000
Less fixed costs	(10,000)	(10,000)	(10,000)
Profit	10,000	15,000	5,000

Company B (£)

		Sales increase 25%	Sales decrease 25%
Sales	100,000	125,000	75,000
Less variable costs	(20,000)	(25,000)	(15,000)
Contribution	80,000	100,000	60,000
Less fixed costs	(70,000)	(70,000)	(70,000)
Profit	10,000	30,000	(10,000)

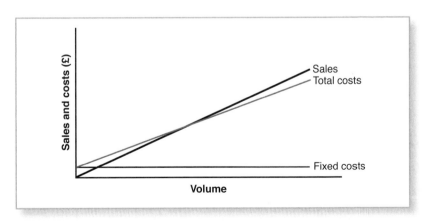

figure 3.4   Company A

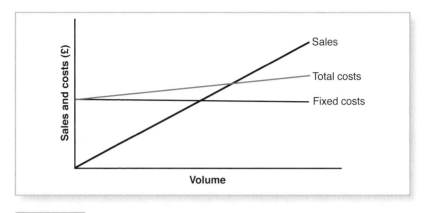

figure 3.5   Company B

Exercise

1 Which company would you rather be with in times of boom? Which in times of recession?

2 Which company is riskier?

The companies illustrate a difference in 'cost structure' (the mix between fixed and variable cost) – see Figures 3.4 and 3.5. This difference in cost structure means a difference in risk and priorities.

Company B suffers more when sales fall because most of its costs are fixed. In the boom times this becomes an advantage as extra sales turn into a lot more extra contribution and consequently profit.

You cannot say one of the companies is riskier than another. Company B is at more risk from changes in sales volume, but company A is at risk from changes in margin. If selling prices decrease slightly for company A, most of its profits disappear. If variable costs increase slightly most of its profits disappear. Company B has far more flexibility with its price. If sales volumes are down then the company can discount prices considerably and still make a contribution. Unfortunately this may well be true for its competitors too and a price war could easily result.

The priority for company A is to focus on maintaining margins and contribution rates; the main focus for company B should be about managing fixed costs and managing volumes. When you are producing your budget it is a good idea to identify the key figures and factors that you need to concentrate on in order to deliver the best performance. Is your company a company A or a company B? How will this affect how you produce your budgets?

Exercise

Review the list of companies below. Try to identify which are more like company A with a low contribution rate and low fixed costs, and which are more like company B with a high contribution rate and a high proportion of fixed costs. Your answer will depend partly on the timescales you consider the costs over. It may be argued that for most businesses, in the very long run all of their costs are variable and that in the very short run many of their costs are fixed.

The answers are given overleaf so don't turn the page until you have attempted the exercise.

Company A or B?

	A	B
Company A Low contribution rate High variable costs percentage	✓	
Company B High contribution rate High fixed costs percentage		✓
1. Hotel chain		
2. Airline		
3. Tour operator		
4. Supermarket		
5. Motor manufacturer		
6. Mobile telecoms		
8. Car rental firm		
10. Power generator (gas)		
11. Power generator (nuclear)		
12. Management consultants		
13. Training company		
14. **Your organisation**		

Company A or B? Answer

	A	B
Company A Low contribution rate High variable costs percentage	✓	
Company B High contribution rate High fixed costs percentage		✓
1. Hotel chain		✓
2. Airline		✓
3. Tour operator	✓	
4. Supermarket	✓	
5. Motor manufacturer	✓	
6. Mobile telecoms		✓
7. Car rental firm		✓
8. Power generator (gas)	✓	
9. Power generator (nuclear)		✓
10. Management consultants		✓
11. Training company	✓	✓
12. **Your organisation**		

Feedback

1. Hotel chain	The main costs of the hotel will be the cost of staff and the cost of the hotel building and its resultant depreciation: these costs are largely fixed. It used to be that if you arrived at a hotel with unsold rooms late at night you could negotiate a discount on the hotel room rate. The development of internet booking has largely removed this opportunity. Websites like LateRooms.com sell unsold hotel room nights at bargain prices. The hotel could discount hotel rates down to their variable costs and still make a contribution. Consider a hotel charging £120 per night. The variable costs of servicing that hotel room could be just £20. If the hotel discounts the room down to just £60 it still makes a £40 contribution that it would not otherwise have received.
2. Airline	The main costs for the airline will be cabin crew, aircraft and aircraft fuel. These costs will be largely fixed. Perhaps there will be a small increase in the amount of fuel used with more passengers but probably most of the fuel is used to raise the weight of the plane. In recent years the most successful new airlines are the budget airlines. These airlines are largely copies of the US company Southwest Airlines and its success may be down to three factors: Southwest Airlines reviewed its services and identified what customers wanted from a shorthaul flight; It eliminated costs that did not add value to customers; Southwest Airlines also motivates its staff well. The key success related to cost structure is the recognition that the profitability of an airline is largely due to maximising the number of flights and aircraft that can be used each day and maximising 'load factors' or how full the aircraft are. One of the most cost-efficient airlines in the world is the Irish budget airline Ryanair. Ryanair's cost efficiency is a direct result of its very high load factors.
3. Tour operator	A tour operator buys flights and accommodation and these may be thought of as variable costs. It only buys the flights and accommodation it needs for the holidays sold. However, the tour operator may well have to buy some of these in advance. In the very short term, many of the tour operator's costs may be considered fixed. This would explain the practice of bargain break and late availability holidays. Many major tour operators also operate their own airlines; however, they will need to be careful to ensure they set their capacity at a level that they can confidently fill. They will contract other airlines at the margins of their business, and by doing this will pay a higher rate for the flights but the risk of having underutilised capacity will be eliminated.

4. Supermarket	When people think about the costs of running a supermarket they often focus on the cost of the stores. The costs of building and operating the stores are quite small in comparison to the cost of the merchandise that the supermarket sells. The key to managing a profitable supermarket is to manage the margins. In a hotel it would not be exceptional to negotiate a 50 per cent discount on the hotel bill but there would be very little chance of negotiating a 50 per cent discount on your weekly grocery bill. Consider a supermarket selling a tin of beans for 40 p: perhaps it is purchasing the beans for 30 p. Assuming it is selling millions of tins of beans, if it can increase the selling price slightly or reduce the purchase price slightly this will have a massive impact on the overall profit. Supermarket buyers are known as hard negotiators!
5. Motor manufacturer	As with the supermarket, when people think about motor manufacturers they often think about their costs for their factories. Typically most of the car (perhaps 70 per cent of the cost) is bought-in materials and components. Like the supermarket the motor manufacturer has to carefully control its selling prices and variable costs. Suppliers are constantly challenged to find cost reductions. Motor manufacturers know the cost of building a car down to the last penny, and if they can make a small saving on each car they will.
6. Mobile telecoms	A mobile telecoms company has a massive investment in its infrastructure and in many cases in expensive 3G and in the future 4G licences. The variable costs to the network operator incurred when you make a call on your mobile phone are generally very small. Mobile network operators want to maximise the revenue from their networks so large customers can negotiate massive discounts by guaranteeing massive volumes.
7. Car rental firm	A car rental firm's main costs are the costs of its cars and staff, both of which are fairly fixed. The key to success within a car rental business is matching the capacity to the demand: unrented cars still depreciate and still need to be financed.
8. Power generator (gas)	A new gas powered station may cost several hundred million pounds to build. The main cost of operating the station is not the depreciation or its capital cost but the cost of the gas fuel. The gas fuel costs are a variable cost as the more the station generates, the more gas it burns. The main risks in operating a gas powered station are the risks that electricity prices go down and gas prices go up. Operators of these stations generally need to 'hedge' or fix gas prices and electricity selling prices in order to guarantee the profitability of the station.

9. Power generator (nuclear)	A nuclear power station is very capital intensive. The newest nuclear power station in the UK (Sizewell B) cost £2.4 billion to build. Apart from the capital costs there are also costs of fuel, reprocessing the fuel and decommissioning the power station and many of these costs are fairly fixed. In order to maximise the profitability of the station the operator needs to maximise the station's output by minimising 'outages' (non-working days) or any factor that reduces generating capacity.
10. Management consultants	The main costs for a firm of management consultants are the consultants' salaries. Like firms of accountants and lawyers, management consultancies are obsessed with the utilisation of their staff. They record staff time and try to maximise billable hours. A consultancy may change its cost structure by utilising contractors, only buying in consultants when they have projects.
11. Training company	Most training companies operate with teams of associates or subcontractors: when they win work they buy in the hours they require to deliver it. If they operate on this model they are a company A – most of their costs are variable. Some training companies will operate with their own team of staff trainers. Training companies using this model would be a company B with most of their costs being the fixed costs of their employees.
12. **Your organisation**	In understanding whether your organisation is a company A or a company B it is important to understand what the most crucial factors to plan, manage and budget are. If you are a company A, you need to focus on your variable costs and contribution rates. If you are a company B you need to focus on your sales volumes, utilisation and fixed costs. If you are having difficulty deciding what your company cost structure is, ask yourself some simple questions. What are our total costs and what proportion are fixed or variable? What is our contribution rate – what is the difference between our selling price and our marginal cost?

Capital expenditure planning

Capital expenditure is about spending money on long-term assets. Long-term assets could be things like plant, machinery and equipment. Capital expenditure could also be about developing products and brands that deliver a long-term return. It normally means spending cash today in order to gain more cash tomorrow.

Plans for capital expenditure must take into account how limited cash is today as well as 'the time value of money' (see Chapter 6). Constructing a capital expenditure plan requires us to produce a model of the cash flows associated with our projects. Further details of capital budgeting are covered in Chapter 6.

4

How should the budget be built?

There are different approaches to building budgets. The three most recognised are known as incremental budgeting, zero based budgeting and activity based budgeting.

What does each approach mean? Which approach is best? How do you go about collecting information and building budgets? How can you get better at forecasting costs and income? How can you work with your finance department to make things better?

Introduction

Before building budgets, it is important to have clear statements about the company's policy, objectives and strategies. We need to know where we are going and what is important to the organisation. Some of the key information will usually be described in the organisation's statements of values, mission and vision.

The key objectives within the organisation may also be further emphasised within a balanced scorecard (see Chapter 9 for more details) or something similar. Before beginning to work on your budgets, be sure that you know what your organisation's objectives and priorities are.

Building budgets

There are many different approaches to building a budget. Some approaches are simple but flawed, others are comprehensive but complex. While the latter might be considered 'the textbook solution' they are often too difficult to use practically.

Budgeting in most organisations takes a long time. According to a study by the Hackett Group in 2008,[1] 73 per cent of major companies take more than three months to produce their budgets. This means the budget is already three months out of date when the year starts.

Finance directors in most organisations believe that the budget building process takes too long and consumes too much time and too many resources. The amount of time and resources that can be justifiably spent on building budgets depends upon how much benefit the activity provides. Spending time and resources to build a budget may well result in long-term savings and benefits.

Studies by the Hackett Group in 2011[2] have identified some practices which can reduce the amount of time and resources required to produce the budget. There are simple steps that can be taken to reduce the amount of work in budget preparation such as reducing needless detail by having too many budget lines or cost centres. We will have a closer look at these within different approaches to budgeting.

Different budgeting approaches

The three main recognised approaches to building a budget are:

- incremental budgeting
- zero based budgeting (developed in the 1970s)
- activity based budgeting (developed in the 1990s).

Incremental budgeting

Incremental budgeting is the simple approach to building a budget. You start your budget with what you did last year and amend it for the changes that you expect for this year. Managers like this approach because it is quick and easy. However, it can be that last year's workload or activity is actually quite different from this year's.

Organisations are often criticised for their rush to spend money at the end of the financial year. You may have witnessed this in your

1 Enterprise Performance Management Research Series, The Hackett Group, 2008–2011.
2 Ibid.

own organisation or in organisations that you work with. The main factor driving this rush to utilise budgets fully is that many managers believe their budgets will be cut if they do not spend them – 'use it or lose it' is the message. This is more likely to be true if the organisation operates a system of incremental budgeting. Rushing to use up budgets invariably means the budget is not used as well as it could be.

Because budgets are not based on plans, it is more likely that managers will hold back part of their budget as a contingency until the end of the year. In doing this they again distort spending patterns and encourage an end of the year rush to use up the budget. Budget expenditure can sometimes be portrayed by a 'hockey stick' shaped graph – flat spending throughout the year rising abruptly at the end of the year.

Incremental budgeting can promote 'budget inertia'. This arises when the budget justifies expenditure, and people do not question how the original budget was built.

Incremental budgeting mistakes

Example 1

Last year, a training manager spent £100,000 on external training courses and consultants. This year, staff numbers are up by 10 per cent so he puts forward a budget of £110,000. (This is the same as last year plus an extra 10 per cent to account for the extra personnel.)

What he has not considered, is that last year the company was faced with new legislation and software changes which meant a lot of extra training was needed. This year there is not the same requirement because most people are already trained. This year's budget should be based on a fully costed training plan that considers actual needs.

Example 2

A site manager estimates the budget for building maintenance by reviewing the expenditure from the previous year. What he misses is the fact that a new contract with a different supplier at a different price has been awarded, and that a different programme of maintenance has been planned for the year.

Example 3

A company calculates a budget for storing archive documents with an external contractor. It reviews the charges and estimates them to be similar to last year, based on the same number of documents being stored. What it needs to consider is that the legal requirement to store some of the archive documents has now expired. However as the storage fees are 'in the budget' no one questions the fact and documents are stored that do not have to be. This is a classic example of budget inertia. See if you can identify any budget inertia in your organisation. Are there some easy savings you could deliver?

Zero based budgeting

Zero based budgeting means starting the budget from scratch. Every line and every cost has to be rejustified. The zero based budgeting approach was developed in the 1970s and promoted by President Carter in connection with US federal government expenditure.

Building a budget from scratch means that all costs should be reviewed and challenged. In order to carry out this exercise fully you need a considerable amount of time and resources. This is difficult when most organisations already believe they spend too much time and money on budgeting. Even with a zero based approach budget setters may be tempted to base some of their cost estimates on previous years.

A compromise may be to complete budgets on an incremental basis (as in the previous examples) and then to periodically review budgets on a true zero cost basis, which requires managers in selected departments to rebuild their budgets from scratch. Some budgets are more usually completed on a zero based basis, for example one-off projects, which by their individual nature will most likely be built up from scratch because they have not been set before.

Activity based budgeting

As already mentioned, activity based costing (ABC) was developed and promoted by Professor Robert Kaplan (of Harvard Business School) in the 1980s. It is an approach that produces more systematic costings based on costing activities.

This activity based approach was extended to budgeting in the 1990s (hence activity based budgeting) with budgets being based on planned activity, which is then converted into a cost based budget on an activity cost model. Few companies have adopted activity based costing so only a small minority would have the data to truly produce their budgets on this basis.

Despite the lack of data, the terminology and concepts of activity based budgeting could still be used to help managers think differently and promote the idea that budgets are not allocations of funds but are actually plans for activities that are going to be performed.

Managers can be encouraged to think about their budgets primarily in terms of activities. What activities are they planning to perform next year? How much do these activities cost? If there are insufficient funds for all the activities they are planning to do, they can then try to find cheaper ways of performing all the activities. Alternatively, they could try to identify the activities that could be cut. In order to cut activities they need to prioritise them and consider which ones are least likely to affect the delivery of the organisation's objectives.

Generally, budgets are based around departments and functions (known as functional budgets). A 'true' activity based budgeting approach focuses not on the departments, but on the activities within the business – these budgets would be cut across departments. Few large organisations' systems would be able to handle this approach.

In most organisations, the budgeting approach has to match up with a system of departmental cost and income responsibility. Even within the framework of a department or functional based budget it is possible to encourage managers to think of their budget more in terms of discrete activities.

Managers do not manage costs, they manage activities – cutting costs means doing less activity or finding cheaper ways of doing the activity. This idea also helps us move away from thinking purely about costs and inputs towards thinking more about activity, outputs and outcomes (i.e. what our spending delivers).

Example: the advantages of focusing on activities rather than on costs

When times are hard and savings need to be made, it can be very tempting to slice a percentage off everyone's budget. An example might be to say that all budgets will be cut by 5 per cent, or there might be a freeze on recruitment or a freeze on overtime. All of these savings are arbitrary and whilst they might appear to be 'fairer' they do not take into account the best interests of the organisation as a whole.

Cutting one department by 5 per cent may affect the whole organisation very badly, whereas cutting another department by 10 per cent may have comparatively little impact. Rather than cutting budgets, organisations should seek savings by cutting activities. The activities which should be cut are those activities that contribute the least to the organisation's achievement of its objectives.

If a budget is built based on a plan of prioritised activities it may be easier to justify and to identify potential savings (should they be required) by cutting activities.

Exercise

Your own budget is probably expressed in terms of lines of expenditure or by account code. Take your budget and try to visualise it instead as being available to perform various activities.

1 If your budget was cut what activities could you cut?

2 How much would be saved by cutting these activities and what would be the impact on your organisation?

Should budgets be top-down or bottom-up?

Budgets may be built from the bottom of the organisation upwards, with each individual department head putting forward his or her own costed plans. This approach ensures a high level of commitment to the budget figures. Although this works for the individual departments, when all the plans for all the departments are added together, the likely result may not meet overall company objectives. Therefore budgets need to have some top-down input (input from senior management) as well.

Top-down budgets are thought of as budgets which are imposed from senior management within the organisation (or the top). This can feel very prescriptive but the top-down input does not necessarily need to describe the budget in detail. Senior managers can use it to give department managers some guidance on objectives and targets. The requirement then for department managers is to produce plans that fit within these constraints.

Research by the Hackett Group[3] investigated the budgeting practices of successful companies. It found that companies which used a predominantly top-down approach were able to produce their budgets much more quickly. Top-down budgets tend to start with the organisation's strategy and objectives, whereas bottom-up budgets may be focused on operational detail and thus become distracted from the bigger picture.

3 Enterprise Performance Management Research Series, The Hackett Group, 2008–2011.

How much detail?

People often assume budgets that are based on plans must be compiled in considerable detail. One could go to enormous lengths to identify a model that covers all costs in great detail but it is not always necessary and much of this detail and effort may be redundant. If the detail in the budget is reduced then the budget can be produced more quickly and with fewer resources.

Example

Simplification measures include:

■ Smaller, less significant lines of the budget could be consolidated into fewer lines.

■ Focus on budgeting for the bigger, more significant costs in the most detail. Try applying the '80/20 rule' – perhaps a small proportion of your budget headings account for the majority of your cost centre or department's expenditure.

■ Rather than budgeting for each employee's payroll costs, calculate the average cost per employee and budget for a total figure based on the number of employees multiplied by the average cost.

Budget simplification does not just happen. Use the following exercise to take some active steps to make an improvement in your budgeting today.

Exercise

1 Review your own budgets.

2 Can you work with your accountants to consolidate some of the lines of your budget?

3 Have you tried to work out any of your costs in too much detail?

4 Can your organisation reduce the number of cost centres?

Fixed v flexible budgets

We may set a budget as a fixed figure for a budgeted volume, but variances will arise if sales volumes are different. It may therefore be better to operate with flexible budgets. A flexible budget adjusts to the changes in volume. We still need to explain variances that arise from changes in volume but it makes the analysis of our costs much easier.

Self-flexing budgets and automatic reallocation for budgets

One of our clients, a tour operator, designed a clever mechanism to 'self-flex' the budgets of resort destinations, managed locally by a resort manager. Resort managers were assigned a notional income which met their total budgeted costs for the resort destination. The income was then related to budgeted sales volumes (people booking holidays at the destination). If sales volumes increased, the notional income increased and resort managers would therefore spend more to deliver their service to customers. If volumes fell, then income fell, and the cost centres would need to find savings in order to meet their budgets.

This clever mechanism automatically reallocated resources to meet demand and allowed managers more resources to deliver the service but required them to make savings when demand fell. Managers did not have to spend the increased budget: they could save part of it and deliver a notional profit against their budget. This would be fine providing they still delivered all of their customer service key performance indicators (KPIs).

Could you develop a similar self-flexing mechanism in your organisation?

External comparison driven budgets

Budgets tend to be cost focused and more about inputs rather than outputs. Ideally budgets will incorporate KPIs. There is a growing movement that suggests performance measures should be related more around external comparisons rather than an internally generated budget.

For example, rather than setting a budget based on a total cost for a department, it could be expressed in terms of a relative performance measure such as the lowest unit costs in comparison to peer group companies. Particular advocates of external relative performance targets are Jack Welch, former CEO of GE, and the 'beyond budgeting movement' (see Chapter 11).

VFM, outcome orientated and evidence based budgets

Cost budgets should be about delivering outputs and outcomes. Ideally budgets should be based not just on what you spend but also on what you deliver. This approach was developed in the UK public sector and is known as 'value for money' (VFM). The output and the resultant outcomes should be proven with some evidence. If you are making a case for a budget, it makes sense to justify your budget in terms of what it will deliver. If you can demonstrate a better likelihood of delivering the results you aim to with some hard evidence, your case will be many times stronger. Differentiating between output and outcomes can be challenging – the output is what you produce, the outcome is the consequence of what you produce.

The main flaw in the VFM approach is that quantifying outcomes is difficult. In some instances it may be impossible as outcomes are only expressed in qualitative terms. Remember that outcome measures should be related to a department or organisation's objectives.

Example 1

A training budget should not be based on an allocation per employee or even an amount to deliver a certain number of days of training. It should be a plan to achieve certain objectives and outcomes. A desired outcome for customer service training might be better customer service resulting in fewer complaints or more sales.

Example 2

A museum may judge its performance partly on the number of visitors it receives (this might be more a measure of 'output' rather than outcome). The museum may have objectives around building and preserving its collections and educating and informing the public. Outcome measures would directly relate to these objectives.

Following public sector cuts, many publicly funded museums in the UK have had to find savings. These savings have mostly come from reducing opening hours. Savings should be made with the minimum impact on the organisation achieving its objectives. Therefore adopt the saving that has the least impact on outcomes.

The power of evidence in protecting budgets

If the relationship between expenditure and outcome can be proven with evidence, making the case for the budget and avoiding future potential cuts becomes stronger. We can always try to learn from the evidence of other organisations, particularly if we work for a public or voluntary sector organisation.

Evidenced based budgets are becoming more important in some sectors such as public healthcare. The accumulation of vast quantities of data and analytical analysis may well make evidence based budgets more common in other areas in the future.

There is a marketing quote attributed to John Wanamaker (1838–1922), a famous US retailer: 'Half the money I spend on advertising is wasted; the trouble is I don't know which half.' Internet advertising allows tracking of campaigns and potentially less waste – but only if we collect and analyse the data (or evidence).

Exercise

1 Think about your own budgets – can you quantify outputs and outcomes?

2 Can you develop measures related to your department's or organisation's objectives?

3 Can you accumulate evidence that demonstrates that your budget is delivering?

Further details of these ideas and VFM are covered in Chapter 7.

Profit centres are normally primarily measured in terms of profit. It may be that even profit centres have other outputs and outcomes that they are challenged to deliver. For example, a branch of a retailer may be measured in terms of its profitability, but it may also have targets to deliver certain levels of customer service and customer satisfaction. In most organisations managers have obligations beyond profit. These include maintenance of brand standards, customer satisfaction and service, health and safety and environmental impact.

Good budgeting practice and ideas for constructing a budget

1 Information gathering

In order to build a budget, it is necessary to have to have some process for collecting information about planned activities and the cost of those activities. It makes sense to design systems that collect this information automatically.

The previous year's performance may give you an indication of likely unit costs and the cost of undertaking various activities. You should be wary though about basing this year's budget exclusively on last year's expenditure because activities and costs do change from year to year.

Try to understand the relationship between costs incurred and the activities performed. Then ask yourself, how did these activities contribute towards the organisation achieving its objectives? Gather evidence that your expenditure is delivering as you expected or that it is delivering VFM.

2 Start with your plan

If the budget is fundamentally a plan then we need to start building our budget according to a plan of what we are going to do and when during the year.

3 Identify the resources you need to deliver your plan

Define the resources you need to deliver your plan in terms of how many people and how long it will take.

4 Activity based

It is a fundamental quality of a good plan and budget that it is built up from activities. This means identifying what the activities will be in the budget year and then assessing what resources will be required to perform these activities.

In your budget you may be making assumptions about the level of activity and how much resource each activity takes. You should be able to justify and preferably document your assumptions. It is by reference to these assumptions that you will be able to explain any variances from the budget later on.

To complete a budget on a true activity cost basis, you would need a detailed plan of activities and details of what the activities cost to perform. Activity based costing has only been adopted in a very small number of organisations, so it is not likely that this information will be readily to hand.

5 Prioritise activities

In conditions of limited resources, activities will have to be prioritised to ensure the most important activities are performed. You should list out your planned activities in priority order. In the event of having to cut your budget you will cancel the lower priority activities. You can also build your activity list to take into account what you can do if extra resources are given to you during the year.

6 Co-ordination and communication

It is really important to ensure that the budget is co-ordinated with the other departments you work with. Communication with these other departments will not only help co-ordination but may also reduce duplication of work.

7 Involving people and commitment

People will generally be more committed to a budget if they have some involvement in its construction. It is best to give managers clear instructions on constraints and objectives to reduce wasted effort and potential disappointment when budgets are finalised. This means starting the budgeting process with a 'top-down' approach with clear direction from senior management.

8 Realistic but challenging

A budget is a plan. Putting in an over-ambitious budget may have adverse effects if it is not achieved. It needs to be realistic. The budget may also function as a target and consequently should also present (an achievable) challenge.

9 Consistency of assumptions

All your budgeting assumptions should be consistent. Assumptions that affect the whole organisation should also be consistent across the organisation. Try to document your assumptions. This will make it easier when you are explaining budget variances while managing the budget. Investing time to build a good budget makes managing it easier.

10 Develop and promote budget templates

Use or create standard budget templates, normally in the form of an Excel spreadsheet. This will help remind you of costs and perform the calculations for you. Build standard templates for use across the organisation to assist consolidations. Discourage people from building their own models as this can lead to confusion and errors. Protect cells in the spreadsheet that contain formulae and 'given' figures.

11 Demonstrate you have thought about your costs and assumptions

Explain your figures – especially when there is a large variation from previous years. Consider adding extra explanatory notes to the budget template. This will help a reviewer to understand your thinking. You may be required to justify your budget figures; so it makes sense to prepare for this justification when you are building your budget.

Tips

- The more meaningful the details, the better.
- Add more detail on big changes from last year.
- Add more detail for bigger numbers!
- Try to challenge your own figures and assumptions.
- Prepare to be challenged by others. State your assumptions: what is the basis for your figures? (Put yourself in the budget reviewer's shoes!)
- Identify the figures and assumptions that you feel are the most important.

12 Involvement

Involve key knowledgeable people who will help you to deliver the figures.

13 Common data

Use common data, assumptions and calculations. Do not recalculate figures that have already been calculated elsewhere in the organisation. Share your experiences with other managers. This will avoid the same discussions and calculations being made several times.

14 Savings mindset

Search for reasons to spend less money as hard as you look for reasons to spend more!

15 Phasing

Try to phase your budget accurately over the year. It is important to avoid simply dividing an annual figure by 12 unless it is genuinely appropriate. Poor phasing will result in monthly variances which you may have to explain every month.

16 Be consistent with organisational and departmental objectives

Remember your budget (or plan) is part of the overall budget for your department and ultimately the organisation. Therefore it needs to be consistent with both the department's and organisation's objectives.

17 Plan ahead and allow time to complete the budget

We often find managers are under time pressure when it comes to building the budget. By setting up procedures ahead to collect information pressure can be reduced. You may recall the 2008 Hackett Group study that suggested the time to build a budget is normally reduced if an organisation operates a system of rolling forecasts.

Now attempt the personal review exercise on budget building.

Exercise

Constraints

- What are the important constraints in your budget?
- How do you manage them?
- Which function drives your budget (e.g. production, sales, finance)?

Sensitivity ('What if') analysis

- What are the key variables in your budget?
- How do you model them?

Managing risk and uncertainty

- What are the biggest risks in your budget?
- How could you represent them in a budget?

Setting budgets for contingencies

Setting budgets for contingencies is difficult and may potentially encourage needless additional spending. This is because contingency budgets may get diverted into other uses as budgets often get spent solely to justify next year's budget.

If contingencies are incorporated into budgets, they should be built and justified on previous experience, or based upon some other evidence that they are required. Contingencies have to be managed – they should be there to cover specific events or situations. If these fail to materialise, the money should not be spent. It would be better to try to avoid contingencies, but have flexibility within the budget that allows managers to call on extra funds from the organisation for unforeseen events.

We have worked with organisations that set contingency budgets based upon expected values. The expected value is the cost of an event multiplied by its probability. This is illustrated in the following example.

Example

The chances of machines breaking down and their repair costs are given as follows:

Event (breakdown) E	Probability P	Cost (£) C	Expected value (cost) P × C
Machine A	0.6	10,000	6,000
Machine B	0.3	2,000	600
Machine C	0.4	1,000	400
Machine D	0.2	3,000	600
Total contingency			7,600

The contingency might be set at £7,600 but this would fail to cover the breakdown of machine A, which is quite likely to break down – a

60 per cent chance. A more practical contingency would be £10,000, which would then be reduced as the chance of the event passed. Managers should be judged on how they manage the cost of the event if it occurs and on the measures they took to reduce its probability or impact.

The challenge process

Budgets often require some form of internal challenge process to encourage managers to think about improving their performance and to think differently about how they do things. It is the budget reviewer's job to challenge these costs and assumptions. Managers should be prepared for this challenge and be able to justify their figures with a robust case. This challenge process does not need to be (and should not be) adversarial, with managers 'fighting' for budgets.

Managers are often reluctant to see their budgets cut. A smaller budget might mean less status or they might believe it will make their job more difficult. Managers should be seeking continual improvement. Rather than fighting to maintain their budgets, they should be putting their efforts into finding ways to reduce them.

There is so much economic and technological change in most markets that it would be unreasonable to think that budgets could be left unchanged from year to year. Managers should be encouraged to challenge their own budgets, to seek improvements and to identify what is changing in the world that will affect their expenditure.

Building budgets and performance measurement

Budgets are often used to measure performance. The result is that managers may be motivated to set budgets or targets that they know they can beat. The focus becomes about beating an internally negotiated target or delivering 'satisfactory' performance rather than delivering best performance. 'Don't beat the budget beat the competition' is the view of General Electric's Jack Welch.

Budgets should be set to encourage and promote the very best performance, rather than just adequate performance. Perhaps one mechanism to see how well we are doing against the best is by direct comparison with other organisations (benchmarking) and/or the competition.

Exercise

1 Does your organisation promote best performance or 'adequate' performance?

2 How could your budgets and performance be benchmarked – internally and externally to focus on a relative performance measure?

3 How could aspects of your company's performance be compared with competitors and similar organisations?

The budget game

In many organisations the budget becomes a game. Managers put forward budgets and plans in the expectation that they will be required to make savings. This may encourage them to build 'fat' into their budgets which can be cut later. Senior managers may well play a similar game, demanding figures beyond their true requirements so they have scope to give budget holders more.

This game playing is the main reason why budgets are criticised. If your organisation is one that plays a 'budget game' you are going to find it very difficult to change the rules and you will probably have to 'play along'.

If you are in a senior management role, you could possibly stop the gaming. This gaming will be reduced if managers are required to present budgets with justifications. A further measure to reduce gaming is to move away from using budgets as the primary fixed target by which managers' performance is measured, moving instead towards using more external and relative targets.

Presenting budgets

Budgets should be about what managers are going to do, not about what they are going to spend. Ideally budgets should relate expenditure to activity. This activity leads to outputs and outcomes which can then be related back to the objectives of the organisation. When presenting the budget try to highlight these relationships.

If the budget gets cut, the consequence is a cut in activity. This can result in cuts in outputs and outcomes and the possibility of not delivering the organisation's objectives. When cuts are made this should be done by minimising the overall impact on the organisation achieving its objectives. To defend your budget you need to demonstrate its importance to the organisation.

Building budgets with spreadsheets

It is very tempting to believe that budgeting is mainly about spreadsheet modelling. It would be possible to construct a detailed model of an organisation using spreadsheets but the effort would have to be worth it. Would such a model lead to better decision making and control of resources?

Spreadsheets, or more specifically Microsoft Excel, are the tools that are most widely used to create budget and forecast models in most organisations. Some accountants now spend most of their time constructing, managing and editing spreadsheets, but are spreadsheet models always the best tools? Has having these handy tools taken over too much? We have already discussed the role of spreadsheets in forecasting (see Chapter 2) and listed some of the problems with spreadsheet models. These same problems also apply to budgeting.

Tips: working with spreadsheets for budgets

- Resist building your own DIY spreadsheets as much as possible; discourage others from doing so too.

- If you do produce your own spreadsheet, design it so it is easy for others to use, understand and audit. This discipline will also reduce the chance of errors. Ask yourself, would this spreadsheet be able to continue in use if I left the business?

- Promote spreadsheet design as being a professional activity rather than something anyone with a computer can or should do.

- Set standards for spreadsheets – keep them as consistent as possible in layout, format and style.

- For complex models divide input, calculation and output into separate sections.

- Keep spreadsheets as clear and simple as possible.

- Design the spreadsheets so key assumptions can be changed easily – for example if a key material price changed, or an assumption about exchange rates, how would this be quickly and easily updated in multiple spreadsheets?

- Encourage peer review to help identify errors.

- Aim to minimise the amount of data that must be entered to reduce work and keying-in errors.
- Make sure spreadsheet data can be easily transferred between systems.
- Protect formula cells and 'given' figures to prevent them being overwritten.
- Impose strict 'version control' so that you know that users are all working with the same model. Date and document any reasons for changes.
- Remind spreadsheet users to keep all confidential data secure. No spreadsheets should be sent outside of the business without prior consent.

Developing your spreadsheet skills

We have made a strong case for you not building your own spreadsheet models, but if you really do need to get to grips with spreadsheets then the best way is to start building one.

Formal training and advice may save you time. Public classroom training courses often contain content that might not be currently relevant to you and anything you do not use soon after the course often gets forgotten and is therefore time wasted. Excel has a vast range of functions which could not be covered on a single training course and it is very unlikely you would remember them all.

As we mentioned in Chapter 2, a surprisingly good source of short, relevant, timely, convenient and free Excel tutorials is to be found on YouTube.com. There are dozens of freelance IT trainers who have made short video tutorials sometimes with workbooks that can be downloaded from their websites.

Try searching YouTube.com for your desired skill. For example if you try searching for 'Making charts in Excel 2007', this gives you around 3,100 results – not all of them will be useful, but there will be some gems to teach you what you need to know in five minutes. You may have experienced colleagues who can also share some tips to save you time.

By using our suggested DIY approach to improving your spreadsheet skills you are demonstrating that you are again taking responsibility for you own personal development (although since you are reading this book you have already demonstrated that!).

re is one very compelling case, however, for your organisation to
nge some formal spreadsheet modelling training for you and your
colleagues. Your organisation should be trying to encourage some
consistency and standards in the design and use of spreadsheets across
departments. An in-house training course that is highly tailored and
targeted could be an excellent way to do this. Before designing the
training, however, the standards first need to be defined.

If you want to start looking after your own development, some useful
and often overlooked Excel tools for you to explore are as follows:

- **Pivot tables** – a tool for analysing and summarising a table of
  data.
- **Goal Seek** – a tool to help you with optimisation. Solver 'works
  backwards' – what do you need to change a cell value to, to get a
  certain result, or to get the minimum or maximum result.
- **Solver** – A tool like Goal Seek but more advanced (supplied as
  an extra add-in to Excel).
- **Scenario Manager** – when you build a model for a budget you
  may want to try several different scenarios to see which works
  best. This prevents you from having to save each scenario as
  a different spreadsheet and ending up with a confusing mess.
  Scenario Manager allows you to save your different scenarios
  within one spreadsheet.
- **Analysis ToolPak** – an add-in of extra statistical tools
  including forecasting tools (introduced in Chapter 2).
- **FORECAST functions** (introduced and described in Chapter 2).

There are of course limits to what you can learn from a YouTube
video or from your colleagues. For advanced financial modelling we
recommend the comprehensive book *Mastering Financial Modelling
in Microsoft Excel* by Alastair Day if you need to take your financial
spreadsheet modelling skills to an advanced level.

Building a budget exercise/illustration

At the end of Chapter 8 we have included an exercise/illustration 'Best
Budget Training Services'. It builds a simple income statement and
cash flow budget and then reviews performance against it. We suggest
however that first you read the intervening chapters.

5

How should cash be budgeted and controlled?

Cash is often said to be 'king'. How can we plan and manage our cash flow?

How can we plan and manage our working capital (stock, debtors and creditors)?

Planning systems and cash flow forecasting

Large organisations often spend huge amounts of money on enterprise resource planning (ERP) systems such as SAP and Oracle. These systems cover a wide range of functions within the organisation including planning, logistics and accounting. Despite this investment, cash flow forecasting, even in very large corporations, is often completed on a basic spreadsheet in the treasury department.

In the 2011 Hackett Group study, the accuracy of companies regarding costs for revenue, profits and cash were analysed. What the study discovered was that the most accurate forecasts were for revenue, then profits and the least accurate forecasts were generally for cash flow. The cash flow forecast is arguably the most critical forecast in the organisation.

Running out of cash means at worst bankruptcy. Even if bankruptcy is not a threat, not knowing your cash position and therefore being unable to forecast accurately means that you cannot get the best returns on your cash balances. Forecasting cash may be the most fundamental activity a company can do.

We have worked with many small organisations that do not have plans or budgets and despite this some of them function surprisingly well. When the global downturn of 2008 came, some of these small firms started cash flow forecasts out of necessity. Suddenly they found cash was in short supply and the banks were not prepared to lend to them, or in fact to most organisations. Customers tried to hang on to their cash longer by delaying payments and suppliers chased harder to get the cash in. Through careful cash flow monitoring, forecasting and management we can improve our chances of survival.

To understand how we can improve cash budgeting and cash forecasting we need to understand the main differences between profit and cash flow (this was covered in Chapter 3). You may remember that the main differences relate to working capital changes, depreciation, capital expenditure and funding. Capital expenditure planning (also known as capital budgeting) is covered in more detail in the next chapter.

We have already discussed some ideas about better forecasting (Chapter 2) and building budgets (Chapter 4). Much of the content of these previous chapters will apply to cash budgeting and forecasting. We also reviewed the two different approaches to presenting a cash flow statement (direct and indirect) in Chapter 3. In Chapter 3 we suggested that the indirect method is the best approach to take for cash flow forecasting and budgeting.

Managing working capital – cash and risk

Managing cash for most organisations is mainly about managing working capital or:

- stock (inventory)
- debtors (accounts receivable)
- creditors (accounts payable).

Stock and debtors tie up cash. There is an opportunity cost – money invested in working capital could be in the bank earning interest. A more pressing issue for most small businesses is that cash is in short supply and borrowing is difficult or relatively expensive. An additional cost of having stock is that it has to be stored.

Working capital also presents a risk to the business and the reasons for this include:

■ Stock can become obsolete or deteriorate, be damaged or stolen.

■ Customers can go bankrupt or dispute their invoices.

■ Creditors may choose to stop supplying if we do not pay to their terms.

To forecast our cash flow we need to model the working capital.

Managing trade debtors (accounts receivable)

Trade debtors (also known as accounts receivable) are the amounts owed by customers to the business. In many instances, trade debtors are a company's largest asset. Gaining better control of trade debtors can, in many cases, massively improve cash flow. In some cases, improvement in speeding up payment can be simple, such as invoicing sooner, improving invoice accuracy and resolving customer disputes quickly.

We can measure and monitor our performance at managing our trade debtors and credit collections with some simple analysis.

Debtor days and days sales outstanding (DSO)

Approximately how many days does it take to receive payments from customers? This can be calculated in a number of ways. The simplest method is to divide the outstanding trade debtors figure by the annual credit sales figure and multiply by 365. A better method is to express the current outstanding debtors (or accounts receivable) as a proportion of recent months' sales, see the following example.

Example

Outstanding debtors (accounts receivable) as at the end of March, £46,000

	Sales (£)
April–December 20X1	140,000
January 20X2	10,000
February 20X2	20,000
March 20X2	22,000
Annual sales (April 20X1–March 20X2)	192,000

DSO = 31 days of March (£22,000), 28 days of February (£20,000)

(£46,000 − £22,000 − £20,000)

$$\frac{£4,000}{£10,000} \times 31 = 13 \text{ days of January} = 72 \text{ total}$$

A simple alternative calculation is:

Total Debtors Value = £46,000 made up of £22,000 (March's sales −
31 days) and £20,000 (February's sales − 28 days) and £4,000 of January's
sales (4,000/10,000 × 31 days − 13 days)

Total DSO = 31 + 28 + 13 = 72 days

The simpler calculation gives a higher figure for debtor days. This is because as sales are rising over the year, the figure is calculated based on the average daily sale rather than on the most recent sales. This may give a misleading picture of how well we are managing our debtors.

An aged debtor analysis

This analysis and presentation shows our customers' accounts by how much they have outstanding over different time periods. A useful addition is an explanation of why the amounts are outstanding and what action is being taken to enable or enforce payments to be made.

Managing stock (inventory)

Managing stock is not about reducing or minimising stock, it is more about *optimising* it. It is possible to have either too much or too little stock – the target is to have just the right amount of stock. Having too little may cause operational and supply problems, having too much means money is needlessly tied up and increases the risk of stock obsolescence and deterioration.

To optimise the stock we first need to become better at planning, forecasting, monitoring and controlling it. The simple step of investing in an efficient stock recording system can provide a big dividend in improving stock management. Does your organisation know precisely how much stock it has and where the stock is stored?

Improving forecasts will help to schedule production and materials planning. Further details of forecasting tools and techniques are covered in Chapter 2.

Just-in-time (JIT)

The motor industry and in particular the Japanese car manufacturers are well known for their efficiency and managing stock on a just-in-time basis. Under the just-in-time system, components and materials are delivered to the production line just as they are needed. This lean and efficient approach has helped Japanese car manufacturers operate more cost effectively, although it has also exposed them to risks. The earthquake in Japan and the floods in Thailand in 2011 both affected the supply chains of a number of motor manufacturers, causing them to question the virtues of running with so little stock.

Strategic approaches to stock management

The need for stock will be reduced if a company can reduce its product range and reduce the number of components in each product. As mentioned earlier, product rationalisation will also help to reduce costs. Product rationalisation opportunities may be identified by conducting Pareto analysis; a very high proportion of sales might come from just a few products. By focusing on these particular few products the company may reduce its product range without having much impact on its sales volumes.

Latest differentiation of products will enable more standardisation in production. Latest differentiation means making products the same and then adding differences at a late stage. A well-known clothing manufacturer produces jumpers in a wide range of colours but the jumpers are all manufactured in the same off-white colour and only dyed at a later stage of production.

Stock management and budgets

Stock levels must be budgeted in order to plan both purchasing and cash flow. Programmes to reduce inventory should be incorporated within the budgeting process. Rather than merely stating that the inventory will be reduced, specific measures should be identified that will aim to reduce inventory to required levels.

A simple way of measuring inventory management performance is to express inventory in terms of 'days' or of inventory turnover.

Calculations

Inventory days	(inventory value/cost of sales) × 365
Inventory turnover	cost of sales (for year)/inventory

These measures may be incorporated within the budgeting and planning process. The measures have similar problems to the debtor days and days sales outstanding (DSO) calculation in that they will be affected by the rise and fall in current sales levels. More importantly, stock levels today will be set to meet future sales rather than past sales.

A better measure therefore would be to express stock in terms of future expected sales. Stock is also made up of a range of items so it is possible to hold a lot of the wrong stock.

Inventory management performance measurement should also include measures of inventory shortage and its impact on the business's operations. Measures could include:

- percentage of on time delivery of orders v target
- backlog of orders.

Managing trade creditors (accounts payable)

You may think that trade creditors or 'accounts payable' gives us a cheap source of finance, but if you delay paying your suppliers you may suffer from poor service or higher prices. Our payment terms with suppliers should be negotiated bearing in mind the impact on both cash and profit.

Some companies choose to pay their suppliers quickly or strictly to terms. By doing this, they can often manage to negotiate better prices. In some industries, many companies rely on suppliers to largely fund their business. Construction businesses, for example, may manage to negotiate some payments from customers in advance and still delay payments to subcontractors. Many construction projects have very low profit margins, but they require very little capital as the projects are funded by the firms' customers and suppliers.

Whatever your business, the period to pay your suppliers and other terms should be actively managed to gain the maximum advantage and also to meet your business objectives.

Trade creditors and accounts payable can be expressed in terms of days just like inventory and trade debtors (accounts receivable). The trade creditors (accounts payable) days calculation is:

Trade creditors (accounts payable)/cost of goods sold $\times$ 365

Tip

In times of cash flow crisis, many companies delay paying their suppliers. One potential warning sign that a company is in difficulty is to look out for a sudden increase in its trade creditor payment days.

Cash flow in a business

Figure 5.1 illustrates the flow of cash in a business. All cash initially originates from either borrowing or shareholder equity (described on the diagram as funding). Cash is invested in fixed assets and working capital. A firm has to pay its staff and suppliers. The suppliers are supplying materials or services; some of these costs will go into the production of goods and ultimately into finished goods. The goods are then sold (hopefully for a profit). If the goods are sold on credit then cash will be tied up in debtors until they pay.

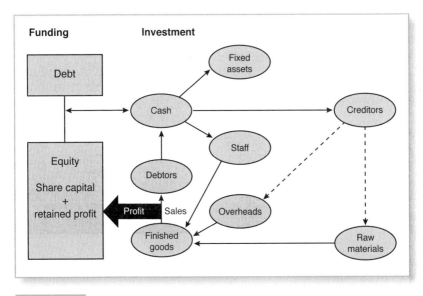

figure 5.1   Flow of cash in a business

6

How should capital expenditure be budgeted for?

In this chapter we will be looking at how investment in fixed assets should be planned and budgeted for. We will also examine how you can budget and plan for capital expenditure.

What is capital expenditure?

Capital expenditure is money that is spent on long-term fixed assets (such as plant and equipment) usually with a view to gaining long-term benefits. Since the expenditure should be giving the company long-term benefits, it should be planned on a long-term basis. In smaller organisations, the main factor determining whether or not a company can invest is whether or not it can afford to!

In smaller organisations, decisions on capital expenditure may well be made on the basis of 'gut feel', with little formal quantification of the expenditure benefits. This does not necessarily mean though that poor investment decisions are made. In larger organisations, capital expenditure proposals normally have to pass some formal tests in order to be agreed. Proposals normally have to include a formal analysis and presentation of costs and benefits. These may be presented as impact on income and expenditure or in terms of impact on cash flow. Building a case for a proposal is a little like building a budget.

Costs can usually be identified more easily than benefits. Quantifying the benefits in financial terms can be difficult and may be a bit subjective. Once the costs and benefits have been quantified, the analysis appears to have some rational objectivity, but the analysis is only as good as the figures that have been estimated. It is not unusual for advocates of a project to be over-optimistic about its costs and its benefits, especially if it is something they are very keen to get.

Getting better at making investment decisions is normally more about getting better at working out a proposal's costs and benefits, rather than getting better at applying some complex investment appraisal model such as discounted cash flow (more details below).

In theory, any capital expenditure that delivers benefits in excess of the 'cost of capital' should be worthwhile. We can think about the cost of capital as being the required rate of return that shareholders want, combined with the cost of borrowing in what is called the weighted average cost of capital (or WACC). Even the largest organisations face problems of 'capital rationing'. This means that whatever their cost of capital is, cash may be limited, and capital expenditure plans have to be made taking into account this constraint.

The payback rule

The simplest and arguably the most commonly used method of investment appraisal is a technique known as payback. Using the payback rule requires projects to pay for themselves within a given period of time. Typically, an organisation might have required all projects to pay for themselves within a period of three to five years.

Following the banking crisis of 2008, many banks restricted their lending, placing cash flow pressures on many companies in the UK. Companies switched their attention from focusing on profits to focusing on cash flow. They tried to manage their working capital, inventory (stock), accounts receivable (trade debtors) and accounts payable (trade creditors) more carefully. They were also forced to review their capital expenditure plans and many companies reduced the required payback period for projects from three to five years down to just 12 months.

Example

The following table represents the cash flows from two potential projects. Each project requires an initial investment of £100,000 and delivers a cash benefit over the following five years only.

Year	Project A (£)	Project B (£)
0 (today)	(100,000)	(100,000)
1	50,000	20,000
2	40,000	30,000
3	30,000	30,000
4	20,000	40,000
5	20,000	50,000
Total	60,000	70,000
Payback	3 years	4 years

Which project would you invest in and why? Project A pays back the soonest in three years, but project B delivers a bigger return overall.

The main benefit of project A is that most of the cash flow returns are in the earlier years. It might be said that there is less risk with project A than with project B. In a real situation we would make a judgement about the risks of each project and their respective cash flows.

NPV and DCF

A criticism of the payback rule is that it puts too much emphasis on quick returns. A project or investment may not pay back within the three to five-year payback period, but may still give long-term benefits which are ultimately worth more to the company.

A better method of investment appraisal is often considered to be the net present value (NPV) or discounted cash flow (DCF) technique. The NPV or DCF technique recognises all cash flows but also takes into account that *cash flows received earlier are worth more than cash flows received later*, due to the time value of money.

The time value of money

Given the choice of receiving £1 today or £1 in 12 months' time, most people would rather have £1 today. If you have to wait for your money it will be affected by inflation and there may be more risk of not receiving it at a future date. Also, if you have £1 today you could invest it and earn a return.

In the following example we assume no risk and no inflation, but that the company is expected to earn a return on cash at 10 per cent and that it pays 10 per cent on funds borrowed (this is a simplified explanation of the company's 'cost of capital').

If we had £1 today we could invest it and have £1.10 in a year, so the promise of £1.10 in a year is only worth £1.00 to us today. £1.00 in a year's time is only worth $1/1.1 \times £1.00$ or about 91p. £1.00 in two years' time will only be worth around 83p to us today. For each year into the future we divide by 1.1, or one plus the cost of capital.

Example

Taking the two projects from the previous payback example, we can take the cash flows and 'discount' them according to the time value of money. The discount factor is a factor to convert a cash value in the future to what it is worth today. The following table provides the discount factors and different rates of the cost of capital together with the formula to calculate the discount factor.

The present value of £1 at different rates of the cost of capital

| Year | Discount rates | | | |
	5%	10%	15%	20%
0 (today)	1.0000	1.0000	1.0000	1.0000
1	0.9524	0.9091	0.8696	0.8333
2	0.9070	0.8264	0.7561	0.6944
3	0.8638	0.7513	0.6575	0.5787
4	0.8227	0.6830	0.5718	0.4823
5	0.7835	0.6209	0.4972	0.4019

Formula

$$\text{Discount factor in year } n = 1/(1 + r)^n$$

where n = year, r = cost of capital

After 'discounting' both projects at 10 per cent, they both have a positive value for the NPV (the sum of the initial investment plus all of the future discounted cash flows). So this means that both are worthwhile projects. At a discount rate of 20 per cent, however, only Project A is worth doing. Discounted cash flow can also be used to calculate a discounted payback period.

Discounted cash flows for Project A and Project B at 10 per cent and 20 per cent

Year	Project A (£)	Project B (£)	Discount rates 10%	Discount rates 20%	DCF 10% discount rate Project A	DCF 10% discount rate Project B	DCF 20% discount rate Project A	DCF 20% discount rate Project B
0 (today)	−100,000	−100,000	1.0000	1.0000	−100,000	−100,000	−100,000	−100,000
1	50,000	20,000	0.9091	0.8333	45,455	18,182	41,667	16,667
2	40,000	30,000	0.8264	0.6944	33,058	24,793	27,778	20,833
3	30,000	30,000	0.7513	0.5787	22,539	22,539	17,361	17,361
4	20,000	40,000	0.6830	0.4823	13,660	27,321	9,645	17,361
5	20,000	50,000	0.6209	0.4019	12,418	31,046	8,038	19,290
Total	60,000	70,000			27,131	23,881	4,488	20,094
Payback	3 years	4 years	Discounted payback		3 years	5 years	5 years	−5,755

Capital rationing: profitability index

The NPV rule indicates whether a project is worth investing in or not. Unfortunately it does not give you any indication of how to rank projects. A simple ranking mechanism is to divide the NPV for a project by its initial investment. This gives you the profitability index.

Assuming that the project investment is limited by the amount of funds available to invest in projects today, then the ranking based on the profitability index will give you an indication of which projects you should invest in first, to give you the best NPV from your limited funds.

Cash budgeting for capital projects is about rationing. Once we have decided which projects are worth investing in we then have to establish what we can afford and when, perhaps by producing a cashflow forecast that may run over several years. Some utilities we work with plan capital projects over decades.

Strategic fit and 'roadmaps'

There is a limit to how far using numerical analysis is useful in making investment decisions. Ultimately we need to use our judgement about the types of projects that are right for us to invest in.

It may be necessary to invest in a project that has a poor NPV or a poor profitability index, because the investment is fundamental to the future success of the business. There may be some projects in which it is not easy to quantify the benefit in financial terms, yet the project may still be viewed as being an essential investment.

When judging projects it makes sense to review them against business plans and strategy. You should ask yourself, 'How will this project contribute to us achieving our long-term objectives?'

In some organisations, management will lay out a 'roadmap' that describes the types of projects they need to invest in to achieve their long-term objectives. All projects can then be evaluated against this roadmap. The question then to be asked is, 'Does the project move us forward to where we want to be or is it, though profitable, a distraction?'

Exercise

1   Does your organisation have a strategy?
2   How does this strategy influence your investment decisions?

3 What type of projects should you invest in today to deliver your business objectives tomorrow?

4 Do you have a roadmap of the types of projects you should be investing in, in the future?

Sensitivity analysis

When putting together a project plan, the list of costs and benefits are only estimates. The analysis and the conclusion will only be as good as the figures that are put into the model. It makes sense to identify the key assumptions behind a proposal, take the key parameters within the project and flex them, testing the project's sensitivity.

One of our clients – a successful UK retailer with over 400 stores – was able to estimate the costs of building new stores and to predict the sales of those new stores with a high degree of accuracy. It was a very cautious company, and within its investment appraisal process it always produced a 'base case' based on its best estimate and then took the sales assumption and varied that to see how low the sales could go before the store was not worth opening. It also reviewed the store's performance with only 80 per cent of the expected sales. This process of taking your key parameters and varying them to see how they affect investment performance is known as sensitivity analysis.

It is possible to make the analysis more complex and sophisticated by varying several parameters and running a simulation known as a Monte Carlo analysis. Making the sensitivity analysis more complex and sophisticated does not automatically make it better – within most investment decisions there are usually only a few key assumptions or parameters to focus on.

Risk

Risk is the probability of an event or situation occurring, multiplied by its impact or cost. With every decision there are risks. When building a business case or putting forward a proposal, all major assumptions and risks around these assumptions should be listed in a risk register. Once they are listed you then need to try to identify the probability of each potential negative event occurring and its likely impact.

It is tempting to focus exclusively on high-probability, high-impact events. This is not always the best thing to do. According to a study by Oxford University and McKinsey,[1] low-probability, high-impact events (sometimes referred to as 'black swans')[2] are often under-estimated, especially in technology projects. The study estimated that one in six major IT projects go over budget by more than 200 per cent.

Exercise

Consider projects within your own organisation. Can you identify any instances of 'black swans' – the occurrence of low-probability events which had a major impact on the project?

Post-investment appraisal

Most organisations fail to undertake post-investment appraisal. The main reason for this is that not many people are interested in the past. Future projects are considered to be more pertinent. Post-investment appraisal though, is probably the most fundamental technique an organisation can use to improve its capital budgeting. By reviewing previous projects you can get better at producing estimates of costs and benefits for future ones.

When projects and investments are reviewed it should be against the original assumptions which were made in the original investment proposal. You can then look at which assumptions were correct, which were incorrect and what can be learned from this experience to make better investment decisions in the future.

Post-investment appraisal has become more challenging in recent years given the pace of change and economic upheavals from 2008 onwards. When making an investment we are normally taking a risk but by reviewing and learning from past projects and situations it should be possible to reduce the risk on future investments.

---

1 Research by Oxford University's Saïd Business School and consultancy company McKinsey & Co., August 2011, **www.ox.ac.uk/media/news_stories/2011/110822_1.html**
2 The phrase 'black swans' was coined because black swans were considered a complete impossibility until discovered in Western Australia by the Dutch explorer Willem de Vlamingh on the Swan River in 1697.

Long-term cash flow planning

In most organisations, capital expenditure plans will be limited by the availability of cash. It makes sense to produce rough estimates of cash flow requirements to cover long-term investment plans. These long-term plans will have to be updated to reflect changing circumstances.

Asset replacement and enhancement

When cash is scarce, it is tempting to delay replacing old assets and to squeeze a little bit more life out of them. By doing this you reduce your cash outflow and your annual depreciation, but you may also lose the benefits of operating new equipment which may have lower maintenance costs and greater efficiency.

Technological change has reduced asset lives in many industries. It is important to plan to replace assets, including forecasting the cost of replacements. It is not possible to predict precisely how technology will change, but it is a fact that change is inevitable and must be planned for as far as possible.

Exercise

1 List out the key fixed asset groups within your business or your area of the business and identify the assets' average age. Can you predict when major replacements are required?

2 Does your organisation have the funds to replace these assets?

3 What other capital expenditure do you need to commit to in the next five years in order to stay competitive within your marketplace?

Investment in working capital

In some projects, working capital investment may be more significant than investment in fixed assets such as plant, machinery and equipment. When making investment decisions, it is important to model the cash flows including the investment in working capital.

For example, suppose we were investing in a new product requiring new plant, machinery and equipment. When we produce a product we will also have to invest in stocks (inventories) of raw materials, work in progress and finished goods. When the product is sold there may be an investment in trade debtors (accounts receivable). The investment in working capital will be reduced by the amount of credit we gain from our suppliers or trade creditors (accounts payable).

Exercise

1 Review a project you have been involved in during the past few years. Within the project was there an adequate understanding of the impact of working capital on the company's cash flow?

2 What would have helped your organisation to model the working capital better?

Remember, you can learn a lot from reviewing previous projects (post-investment appraisal). These reviews will help you to build more comprehensive business cases in the future.

Checklist

If you are involved in investment decisions, use this short checklist when you start to work out your figures:

1 Check the decisions against objectives and policy. For major or long-term decisions demonstrate the 'strategic fit'. Proposals that demonstrate a clear link to company objectives are more likely to be successful. Save your time and effort – there is no point in investing time developing proposals and business cases which are not clearly in line with the organisation's objectives, policy or strategy.

2 Try to quantify all costs and benefits in financial terms. Costs and benefits should be from the point of view of the organisation and not the department.

3 Learn from your experience. You can improve business cases and proposals by looking back at previous decisions to see what went right and what went wrong.

4 Review previous decisions – use post-investment and decision appraisal. In most organisations there is not enough post-investment appraisal. Managers tend to be more interested in new proposals than the ones that have already

passed. There are valuable lessons to be learned from the projects we have already started or completed and these should not be ignored.

5   State and document all assumptions and specify where your figures come from in your proposal. By doing so, you stand more chance of proving the figures to yourself first and providing a convincing business case to the proposal reviewer. When the project is reviewed you can go back to these original assumptions to see which were valid. Doing this may well help to improve future business decisions.

6   Identify 'milestones' for monitoring projects and proposal progress. When we are delivering the project it is useful to have milestones in order to be able to measure and manage progress.

7   Identify critical success factors. For example, what will cause the project or proposal to fail and therefore what needs to be managed?

8   Recognise and try to quantify main risks. There are risks in all projects. You can try to list them according to their likelihood and their impact. Then for each significant risk, think about how you can either reduce the chance of it happening or reduce its impact. Low-probability, high-impact risks are often the ones that are the most overlooked.

9   Include sensitivity analysis (flexing the key assumptions in your business case/proposal).

10   Consider relevant costs and ignore previous sunk cost. Sunk costs are those costs that have been and gone. You want to consider future costs only as you cannot 'unspend' past costs.

11   Gain commitment to the figures through involvement. Involve the people who will be delivering the project in producing the business case. They will then be more committed to the figures.

Managing your budget and delivering performance

7

Back to basics: living within your means and delivering VFM

There are some simple principles to start off managing your budget. In this chapter we provide some simple models to keep you on the straight and narrow.

Budget feedback mechanism

Budgetary control systems need to deliver effective feedback. This feedback tells budget holders what is going on and alerts them to problems. The sooner a problem can be identified the better. Ideally systems will alert budget holders to problems in advance. We should aim to design leading indicators (giving advanced warning) rather than lagging indicators (finding out after the event). Managers should also plan for likely adverse outcomes and have back-up remedial actions.

For example, when you become thirsty your body is giving you feedback that you are dehydrated and you need a drink. This feedback is not necessarily all that useful if you happen to be in the middle of the desert with no water! It makes sense to prepare for likely outcomes by looking back at past experiences. Experiences (and good learned practice) should be shared.

In most organisations and with most budgets the most basic feedback is drawn from a comparison between the original budget and actual expenditure. This feedback is, of course, limited by the quality of the original budget.

Example

A budget manager in Northern Europe builds a budget for utility costs for a full year. He divides the total by 12 to determine a monthly budget. In the winter months he appears to be overspent and in the summer months he appears to be making savings. His colleague is managing an air conditioned factory in the Middle East. She finds that she is making savings in the winter and is overspent in the (hotter) summer months. These variances may have arisen because of poor phasing of the budget – the monthly feedback is providing this information.

One alternative may be to compare the expenditure for the current period against expenditure for the same period the previous year. This seems sensible but does not take into account changes in unit costs or changes in activity. A better indicator of track is to use a 12-month rolling average and see if the average is rising or falling.

To do a rolling average you take the expenditure from the line of cost or a department and divide by 12. You then compare this cost against the previous 12 months' rolling average cost. A comparison can be made to see if generally costs are rising or falling.

Budget figures can be corrupted. If managers know their performance will be measured against a budget then they have a vested interest in manipulating that budget. They may change the budget to make their own performance look better in order to reduce the risks of failing. Where possible, performance measurement should always include external measures or measures of relative performance, for example, comparison against other departments or companies.

Feedback mechanisms should alert managers to take action. A simple presentation of key performance indicators (KPIs) is in the format of a 'traffic light 'or RAG (red, amber, green) status. The results from each measure are presented as:

■ green – performance is satisfactory

■ amber – caution needed, or

■ red – action required.

It is important to limit the RAG status items to a manageable number, and focus the attention of managers on identifying problems and taking corrective action in areas that matter most in the organisation's achievement of its ultimate objectives.

Ratios and budgets

We can use financial ratios to help us monitor our performance and highlight potential issues within our budget.

Example

A retailer may have an expectation of delivering a specified gross margin. The gross margin is the gross profit (sales minus cost of sales) divided by sales; this is normally expressed as a percentage. If the gross margin falls below the budgeted level this may indicate a problem. Many retailers also closely monitor payroll costs against sales as a key control ratio. If sales are down, staff costs have to be reduced; if sales are up, staff are not necessarily increased!

What type of ratios might you use to help you to manage your budget?

Exercise

Review the cost centre report below.

1 How well is the budget manager doing at managing her budget?

2 What other information do you need?

Cost Centre 101	Month/Period 9		
	Actual	Budget	Variance
Payroll	10,000	9,500	(500)
Agency staff	2,000	1,000	(1,000)
Consultancy	1,500	0	(1,500)
Travel	250	100	(150)
Stationery	300	200	(100)
Printing	250	300	50
Total	14,300	11,100	(3,200)
Total overspent against budget		(29%)	

Review of Cost Centre 101

It is impossible to say how the cost centre has done. The cost centre manager has overspent the budget for the month, but we have no details about what the cost centre has delivered or the problems it had to cope with. A cost centre that overspends and delivers its objectives may be said to be better managed than one that underspends and fails to deliver its objectives. Overspending a budget is not necessarily bad; overspending a budget without justification is.

The report only covers a single month. Our view of performance may be corrupted by something happening late or early against a budget that may have been produced over a year earlier. A better review would be to focus on year to date (YTD) performance. Looking backwards over the month and the year to date may encourage us to be reactive while it is far better to aim to be proactive. This may be achieved by reforecasting the full-year results and comparing that to the annual budget. Always try to predict variances rather than discover them after the event as this will give you more time and options to come up with a remedy.

Take a look at the extended report with the YTD and the full-year forecast opposite. In month 9 the cost centre was 29 per cent overspent, while for the full year the cost centre manager believes it will be just 2 per cent overspent.

Over 84 per cent of the cost centre's budget is payroll and this is also where most of the variance has come from. Generally by managing a few big costs carefully we can deliver our budget. As most of the cost centre's costs are payroll this is also probably where the cost centre manager should be focusing her attention. She should consider whether each staff member is delivering all he or she should be according to salary, rather than worrying too much about the stationery costs.

Managing budgets

There is no book or course that can tell you *exactly* how to manage your own budget. You have been given the budget because with knowledge and experience you are the person best qualified to manage it. We have put together the checklist on pages 130–3 to help guide you in your decision making.

Cost Centre 101 Report with YTD and forecast against full year

Cost Centre 101	Month/Period 9			Year to date (YTD)			Forecast	Full Year Budget	Variance
	Actual	Budget	Variance	Actual	Budget	Variance			
Payroll	10,000	9,500	(500)	87,000	85,500	(1,500)	117,000	114,000	(3,000)
Agency staff	2,000	1,000	(1,000)	10,000	9,000	(1,000)	12,000	12,000	0
Consultancy	1,500	0	(1,500)	2,000	2,000	0	3,000	3,000	0
Travel	250	100	(150)	1,100	900	(200)	1,500	1,200	(300)
Stationery	300	200	(100)	1,900	1,800	(100)	2,400	2,400	0
Printing	250	300	50	2,400	2,700	300	3,300	3,600	300
Total	14,300	11,100	(3,200)	104,400	101,900	(2,500)	139,200	136,200	(3,000)
Total overspent against budget			(29%)			(2%)			(2%)

The 13 steps to better budget management

1 **Identify and concentrate on the main income and costs that matter**. Focus your attention on the lines of the budget that matter most. You may start by applying the 80/20 rule: maybe 80 per cent of your budget is down to just 20 per cent of the budget lines or accounts. (The budget lines are the cost or income headings in your budget.)

   Managing these large budget lines carefully will normally have the biggest impact overall. Managers often make the mistake of focusing on costs where they feel they have the most discretion. We may have lots of choice and a lot of chances to reduce expenditure on stationery but normally it is not meant to have much impact on our overall performance.

   In many departments, the largest budget is the payroll cost. Often people imagine they have no control over these costs and that they may as well ignore them. If most of your cost in your budget is payroll, this means that most of your time should be spent making sure that you get the most out of your staff. An hour of time spent on cost control on a petty cost may be better spent managing your staff and getting them to deliver more.

   Labour is not always the main cost. We know of a European manager in a Chinese factory who was surprised at the high level of staff employed to inspect for defects. He wanted to reduce the headcount, but the savings in staff costs were relatively low in comparison to the savings on materials from quality improvement. In many Chinese businesses, even with rising pay rates, material is the key cost to control.

2 **Identify key factors driving main income and costs and monitor them**. After you have identified your main costs, you need to identify and understand the factors that drive these costs. (Remember the ideas discussed in Chapter 3 concerning cost behaviour and ABC.) Could you monitor these factors better?

   The better you understand what ultimately drives your costs, the better chance you have of managing and reducing them.

3 **Identify problems as early as possible – look for early indicators of problems**. The sooner you identify a problem the more options you have to manage it. Can you predict

what your income or costs will be before you get to the month-end? Try to use 'leading' KPIs rather than 'lagging' KPIs to give you an early warning. Rolling forecasts and forecasting (covered in Chapter 2) encourage and enable you to be more proactive and less reactive.

4 **Check monthly variance reports and** *explain* **important variances from budget – use tolerance limits to identify important variances**. The difference between actual performance and budget performance is the variance and there are more details about variance analysis in the next chapter. The key to good use of variance analysis is not calculating variances but explaining them, getting to the underlying cause and identifying action. Explaining the variances normally means returning to the original assumptions within the budget and establishing what was different and why. We can employ a technique known as root cause analysis.

5 **Analyse trends**. We must identify whether variances are an on-going problem and possibly part of a trend or are they a one-off hiccup? Looking at the variances for the year to date rather than just the month will be more likely to help identify trends.

6 **Be aware of phasing (timing) differences between budgets and actual spending**. When we construct the budget we should try to phase it as accurately as we can over the year. Every month though, we will have variances that arise purely because costs or income have arisen at a different time from when they were budgeted for. It is important to be aware of these variances and to be able to explain and allow for them.

7 **Reforecast income and expenditure and then, if required, take corrective action as soon as possible to meet the original budget**. In Chapter 2 we covered the importance of forecasting and some tools and techniques to help you produce forecasts. Regular forecasting is an important tool for helping us to manage budgets and replan during the year.

8 **Allow time to manage the budget – see the budget as being more than a monthly financial report**. Managing the budget takes time. In some managers' eyes the budgets are seen as an administrative burden. The role of the budget and its importance should be promoted to budget managers so that

they devote appropriate time to this important activity. Try not to think of budget management as being an activity that you do when you sit down with your reports at the end of each month, but as the sum of your management activity over the month. Decisions you make within your job will ultimately end up in the financial report at the end of the month. To some degree you could say you are always managing your budget.

9 **Trust your judgement – you have the budget because you are the expert**. You are managing a budget with every decision you make within your work. You have been given the budget that you have because *you* are the best qualified individual to make decisions over that part of your organisation's activities.

10 **Drill down on reports: total – detail – transaction – source**. In many reporting systems there is an option to 'drill down' and get more information behind the costs recorded in your department. By drilling down you will normally be able to get to the individual transactions that make up the total costs within any given line of your budget. Some of these transactions you will find confusing as they will not relate to accounting adjustments or often 'accruals'. Try to focus on identifying the transactions that you are responsible for and ensuring that your cost centre is being correctly charged for costs that belong to it.

11 **Be aware of errors and miscoding**. In all organisations there are errors and miscoding. When we review our financial reports and find a significant error we should ask our accountants to correct it. Making these corrections takes time and resources. You may find errors which are too small to have any significant impact on performance, and it is better for the organisation as a whole if you disregard these. It is always disappointing to be charged a cost to your department which does not belong to you, but try to ignore it and focus on the income and costs that really matter. If, though, you discover that the same small errors are appearing every month, contact your accountants and ask them to investigate and correct this recurring problem.

12 **Work with your finance colleagues**. The finance team in your organisation is there to support you so make it easier for it to support you by supporting it. Send the team feedback on your budget performance and warn it of any

known upcoming problems as soon as possible. Do ask the finance team questions and aim to understand the answers so you will not be asking the same question next month.

13 **Seek to manage value and cost**. See the next section on value for money.

The VFM model for managing and planning budgets

We introduced the value for money (VFM) model in Chapter 3. This is a model developed in the UK public sector by the Audit Commission. Public bodies are required to demonstrate that they are delivering VFM. The model has some deficiencies but it still provides a useful way of thinking about budgets and, more importantly, a way of communicating what budgets are about and seeking improvements in performance.

Often managers and organisations focus on inputs when they are setting and reviewing budgets. The VFM model seeks to encourage managers to think about outputs and, more importantly, outcomes. Outcomes are the consequences of our expenditure. This way of thinking is especially useful when considering budgeting in cost centres which tend to be more input orientated.

Costs – the input (costs, or budgets, buy resources)

Resources (resources deliver outputs)

Outputs (outputs deliver outcomes)

Outcomes – the consequence of the expenditure

Differentiating between outputs and outcomes can be difficult. A training manager may aim to deliver better VFM by delivering more training days (output); however the consequence of what the training results in is the outcome.

Exercise

Take your own budgets and list out:

1 Your main cost headings.

2   The main resources that you purchase – this will often be staff
    time.

3   The outputs delivered by the resources. Can these be
    quantified and measured?

4   The outcomes you are seeking to achieve. Can these be
    quantified and measured?

The three Es

The VFM model breaks down into three methods to find improvement:

- **Economy** – buying resources more cheaply. For example, buying
  supplies, contractors and employee hours at a cheaper rate,
  but remember that the cheapest is not always the best option.
  Economy can be described by the formula: resources/cost.

- **Efficiency** – delivering more output from resources. For
  example, squeezing more output from contractors or employees
  for the same total cost. Efficiency can be described by the
  formula: output/resources.

- **Effectiveness** – delivering better outcomes from the output.
  For example, not just delivering more output but getting a
  better overall end result for the customer or the organisation.
  Effectiveness can be described by the formula: outcome/output.

Overall VFM can be described by:

$$\text{Economy} \times \text{efficiency} \times \text{effectiveness} = \text{VFM}$$

and

$$\text{Resources/cost} \times \text{output/resources} \times \text{outcome/output} = \text{outcome/cost}$$

To maximise VFM, you have to maximise the outcome/cost. The flaw
in this formula is that general outcomes cannot be quantified.

Evidence: proving VFM

A fourth and vitally important 'E' not included in the original
model is 'evidence'. To demonstrate VFM we must prove our efforts
are delivering an outcome. Evidence based decisions are becoming
increasingly important in the public sector, particularly in healthcare.
In most organisations, justifications for expenditure with evidence of
outcomes are much stronger. Collecting evidence may also help you
to justify budgets in the future.

Example

One of our clients is a major British police force that undertook a campaign targeting burglars. As a part of the campaign it used extensive poster advertising. The posters were not aimed at burglars, but rather they were aimed at the general public. So what was the purpose of the posters?

Traditionally, when people are asked what the police should spend their money on they will invariably answer 'more police officers'. Perhaps by seeing more police officers on the streets, members of the public feel reassured. The cost of this advertising could perhaps have been used to employ a few more police officers, but in fact this change in the number of police officers would hardly have been noticed. By spending the money on the posters, a greater impact in terms of public reassurance could be delivered.

To judge the decision in terms of was it good VFM or not it must be measured against the objectives that the expenditure was trying to achieve. By spending on the posters rather than on extra police officers the force may well have been able to deliver greater VFM.

A key element in determining what is VFM is measurement. You need to be collecting evidence that the expenditure is delivering the outputs and outcomes that it should be.

A modified VFM model

In Figure 7.1 we have modified the VFM model to include 'capacity' as a consideration. Resources and cost can be reduced, but as we do so we may be reducing our capacity. Minimum cost may be achieved by maximising capacity utilisation, but by doing so we may be taking a risk of being unable to meet demand. We have also added the fourth 'E' – evidence – to remind you that we should always be seeking to demonstrate that we are delivering a return from our expenditure and always asking how the expenditure contributes to our objectives.

Exercise

1 Could you reduce cost by reducing capacity?

2 Can you reorganise your resources (mainly personnel costs in most organisations) to be more flexible between peaks and troughs of demand?

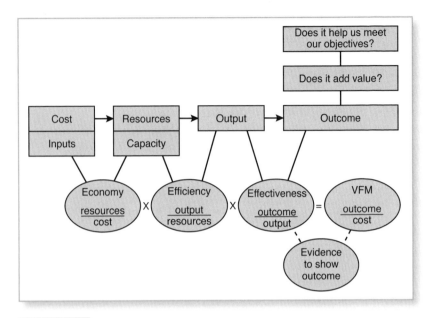

figure 7.1   The modified VFM model

Cost savings

Building and managing budgets should not just be about automatically finding cost savings, but managers often have an annual target to do just that. If you are trying to find savings remember they should not be at the expense of value, outcome or the end result.

Exercise

It is very difficult to construct a universal list of cost savings for all departments in all organisations. The following list is intended to prompt you to think about some practical approaches to manage and reduce your costs. Why not take the list and work through it with your team?

	Notes *Your practical application and thoughts*
Look for 'better costs' not necessarily less costs. Sometimes extra cost adds more value. When looking at cost look at value as well.	

Cost reduction should never be an end in its own right. Any exercises in cost reduction should be considered against how the action affects us reaching our objectives (e.g. gaining a sustainable competitive advantage, delivering shareholder returns, maintaining corporate stability).	
Think and work smarter not harder! Perhaps this is a modern management cliché, but in many organisations people are already working extra hours beyond their contracts so focus on the amount of work rather than the outcome (result).	
Can we use a different (innovative) approach? Where can we learn new ideas?	
Can we benchmark ourselves? Who can we compare our performance against internally or externally? Who is the best in the world and why?	
The costs of activities may be measured. The value of activities is a management judgement. What activity keeps you or your team busy but delivers little apparent benefit?	
Cost reduction may also focus on finding cheaper ways to perform activities. Costs may be reduced by cutting out activities or reducing complexity, but in doing so it is important to consider the value of what has been given up.	
Reducing small costs gives small rewards. Therefore it is better to concentrate on the large controllable costs.	
Encourage cost consciousness in others (but preferably not meanness). This may be done by appropriate delegation of cost responsibility.	

	Notes *Your practical application and thoughts*
When delegating cost responsibility try to include responsibility for failure costs – the cost of things going wrong.	
Recognise the potential costs of over- and under-specification.	
Never be arbitrary about cost reduction or budget cuts. Always be deliberate. Examples of arbitrary budget cuts include general freezes on overtime and recruitment and across the board percentage budget reductions.	
Better planning now may save costs in the long run. For example, what plant and equipment will the job/ contract need? Organising it now may mean we can obtain it at a cheaper price.	
Plan (for change!). Try to avoid cutting costs in a crisis. Try to predict problems and be proactive rather than reactive. Identify possible savings and priorities early.	
When delegating cost management ensure the team is clear on the organisation's and department's aims, objectives and priorities.	
In some instances costs may be reduced by resource substitution. This is replacing resources with cheaper ones.	
Identify and reduce duplication of effort and activities.	
Identify slack resources and release them to other parts of the organisation.	

Cost management is for the benefit of the organisation, not the division or department.	
Avoid making savings at the expense of other divisions/areas/ departments, but do make other divisions/areas/departments responsible for their costs.	
Promote and copy successful cost reduction ideas.	
Learn from experience. Understand and explain cost variances.	
Plan costs, and reforecast throughout the year or contract. Concentrate on getting the main costs the most accurate.	
Work with customers and/or suppliers to find joint savings.	
Work with other non-competing organisations through 'strategic alliances'.	
Work towards continuous improvement. Even if your organisation is the best, others are getting better, so you aim to improve as well.	

8

Making sense of standard costing and variances

You may be using a standard costing system and initially this can be confusing. How can you make sense of variances and manage them effectively?

Making sense of variances

Variance analysis is the process of reviewing and explaining the differences between the original budget and actual performance. One might believe that the original budget is always the 'right' answer, but this is a figure that may have been derived 18 months earlier and is now out of date. By making reference to the original assumptions in the budget it may be possible to explain and manage performance better. Variance analysis should not be about assigning blame but about understanding reasons.

One technique that can be applied is known as 'root cause analysis'. In this you ask the question 'why?' several times over – the ultimate aim is to get to the root cause of the variance.

Standard costing

Standard costing is a system of costing where production units are valued at a standard cost. The difference between the actual costs incurred and the budgeted or standard costs of production is the variance.

If you operate a system of standard costing, the calculation of variances can be automated. Calculating the variance is only half the story, what is more important is the cause of the variance. Once we determine the cause it is then possible to work out some corrective action to manage the variance.

Standard costing works well in businesses that manufacture large numbers of the same products. It is poor for businesses that produce bespoke products.

There are a number of criticisms of standard costing including:

- It may be difficult to establish exactly what a cost should be.
- The standard cost may be manipulated to present a challenging or easy target.
- Costs and circumstances may change. Standard costs may quickly become out of date, particularly with volatile commodity prices and changing material costs.
- Standard costs may be used for decision making. If the standard is incorrect, the wrong decision may be made.

In many industries where standard costing may be appropriate there tends to be a high level of automation or standard processes resulting in very little variance in labour costs.

With most of our manufacturing clients the key variance is normally purchase price variance (PPV). This is the difference between the price of materials in the standard and the actual price.

Breakdown of variances

The full breakdown of variance depends on the approach to costing (particularly in relation to overhead recovery). Often complex variance analysis ends up leaving managers confused. Reports that are confusing are more likely to be skipped over. We recommend you keep the analysis simple and focus on the biggest variances that can be managed.

A simple breakdown of variances is as follows.

Sales variances

- **Sales price** – average selling prices are higher or lower than budget.
- **Sales volume** – lost or gained profit from sales volumes is higher or lower than budget.

■ **Sales mix** – mix of sales of products is different from expected resulting in different gross margins.

Labour

■ **Labour rate** – labour rate per hour more or less than budget.

■ **Labour usage** (efficiency) – more or fewer labour hours used than there should have been for the volume of production.

Materials

■ Materials price.

■ Materials usage.

Overheads

The analysis of overhead variance can be complex if you recover absorbed overheads in product cost (see Chapter 3 for a description of overhead recovery). You can simply ask yourself whether the total overheads are more or less than they should be and why.

Tips

1 Referring to a variance as being either positive or negative can sometimes be ambiguous – it is better to refer to variances as either favourable or adverse.

2 Explain variances in order to manage them, not to blame people! The process of explaining the variances might help to detect errors. Try the previously described root cause analysis technique. Ask the question 'why?' several times to try to get to the underlying cause.

Example

Agency staff costs are over budget:

■ Why? Agency staff costs were increased to cover staff absences at a busy time.

■ Why were there staff absences? Because staff were attending a training course.

■ Why did they have to attend at a busy time? Because …

Simple variance analysis example

Barry's Boxes

Barry's Boxes manufactures special boxes for the electronics industry. Each box has the following expected or standard cost:

Labour	3 hrs @ £5 per hour =	£15
Materials	2 kg @ £3 per kg =	£6
		———
		£21
		———

Each month the company expects to manufacture 100 boxes.

The budget for a month was:

Labour	£1,500
Materials	£600
	———
	£2,100
	———

The actual costs were:

Labour	£1,860
Materials	£630
	———
	£2,490
	———

Question
What might have caused the difference between the actual cost and the budget?

The higher expenditure is not necessarily bad. It may well be that the company manufactured more boxes. When we compare actual costs against the original budget we need to flex the original budget to the volume of products produced.

Over the month, 100 boxes were made as planned.

The labour costs were made up of 310 hours @ £6 per hour. (10 more hours were used than should have been; labour was paid at £1 extra per hour.)

The materials costs were made up of 180 kg @ £3.50 per kg. (20 kg less of materials was used; the material cost an extra £0.50 per kg.)

Question
Can you explain the variance below?

	Actual A	Budget B	Variance B–A	
Labour	£1,860	£1,500	(£360)	overspend
Materials	£630	£600	(£30)	overspend
	£2,490	£2,100	(£390)	overspend

Answer

Labour rate variance	£1 × 310	=	(310)	overspend
Labour usage variance	£5 × 10	=	(50)	overspend
			(360)	overspend
Materials price variance	0.5 × 180	=	(90)	overspend
Materials usage variance	3 × 20	=	60	underspend
			(30)	overspend

Analysis

■ Overtime had to be worked because of a machine breakdown.
■ Extra hours were caused by idle time while the machine was repaired.
■ The price of materials was increased unexpectedly as supplies became limited due to a dock workers strike.
■ Better training has paid off with reduced wastage causing a lower than expected materials usage.

We could focus on the numerical aspect of variance analysis, but what is really more important is what caused the variance in the first place and how it can be managed.

Knowing that we have a labour rate variance or materials usage variance tells us nothing if we cannot understand why the variance has arisen. Once we have understood we can take some actions to manage it.

Knowing that the labour rate variance was caused by overtime worked because a machine broke down, and labour efficiency was reduced for the same reason, tells us that we should possibly be spending more on maintaining our machinery.

Practical variance analysis without standard costing

Even without standard costing we will still have variances that need to be explained. Do not focus on calculating variances. Focus on explaining them and identifying suitable corrective action. Variance analysis is not about complex maths, nor is it about making excuses. It is about identifying problems and taking courses of action to solve them.

Following the global economic crisis of 2008, many firms experienced a fall in sales. Perhaps in many businesses the monthly variance analysis reports explained the sales variance as being down to external factors that they could not manage.

Further investigation of the variances may have indicated which types of products and customers were most affected by the crisis. Perhaps this analysis might then suggest where a firm could refocus its efforts to gain sales out of the least-affected sectors and products?

Variance analysis (with or without standard costing) has many of the general problems associated with budgets. The main issues are:

- Comparisons are being made against an internally generated target.
- The variances are historical, encouraging a reactive approach.

It would be better to attempt to judge performance against external measures. Then to try to make the analysis more forward-looking, predicting problems ahead of time to come up with some early solutions.

Exercise

Best Budget Training Services is a new training business starting in December of the current year 20X2, with the first year of their budget running from January 20X3.

■ Part 1 – read the assumption for the year below and create a budgeted income statement and cash flow for the company's first year of trading.

■ Part 2 – review the company's performance for October 20X3 against the budget and then review some of the key variances to be investigated.

Answers for both parts of the exercise are provided, so you can also use it for training or to check your own methods.

Part 1: business description/assumptions

The company plans to run training courses in hired venues with freelance trainers who are only paid for the courses they deliver. Each course should run with around 10 delegates (participants). The overheads will be kept low as the owners (the only employees) will take a small salary each; they operate the business from their home. In the first year they hope to make a small profit.

Part 2: Review

After 10 months of trading the business has been performing badly. The income statement analysed against the budget and latest forecast is given on p. 151. What do you think are the key variances and issues for the owners to focus on?

Profits are down, because sales are down and costs are up against budget. The company has fewer delegates on its programmes and is charging less per delegate. The budget fee for a delegate was £250, the average for October is only £220. Even though sales are down the company is running more courses than budget, causing the per course cost to rise. It is also spending more per delegate.

Fixed costs are above budget; this is mainly down to increased spending on promotion. To explain this variance we would need to compare the original plan for promotional spending against the actual spend.

Best Budget Training Services
Budget plan and assumptions

	Jan	Feb	Mar	April	May	June	20X3 July	Aug	Sept	Oct	Nov	Dec	Total
Planned courses	1	2	3	5	6	7	5	2	6	6	6	3	52
Expected delegates	10	20	30	50	60	70	50	20	60	60	60	30	520

3 courses with 30 delegates in total are expected for January 20X4

Expected costs/income £

Fee per course place 250

Fees are paid by customers one month in advance

All costs except rent and promotion are paid in the current month. Rent is paid annually in January and promotion is paid one month in arrears

Costs varying per delegate

Delegate materials 5

Refreshments 20

Costs varying per course

Venues 300

Trainers' fee 500

Monthly fixed costs

Sales staff 1,200

Admin. staff 1,500

Rent 1,000

Promotion 2,000

Best Budget Training Services
Budgeted income statement (£)

	20X2 Dec	20X3 Jan	Feb	Mar	April	May	June	July	Aug	Sept	Oct	Nov	Dec	Total
Planned courses		1	2	3	5	6	7	5	2	6	6	6	3	52
Expected delegates		10	20	30	50	60	70	50	20	60	60	60	30	520
Sales revenue		2,500	5,000	7,500	12,500	15,000	17,500	12,500	5,000	15,000	15,000	15,000	7,500	130,000
Costs varying per delegate														
Delegate materials		(50)	(100)	(150)	(250)	(300)	(350)	(250)	(100)	(300)	(300)	(300)	(150)	(2,600)
Refreshments		(200)	(400)	(600)	(1,000)	(1,200)	(1,400)	(1,000)	(400)	(1,200)	(1,200)	(1,200)	(600)	(10,400)
Costs varying per course														
Venues		(300)	(600)	(900)	(1,500)	(1,800)	(2,100)	(1,500)	(600)	(1,800)	(1,800)	(1,800)	(900)	(15,600)
Trainers' fee		(500)	(1,000)	(1,500)	(2,500)	(3,000)	(3,500)	(2,500)	(1,000)	(3,000)	(3,000)	(3,000)	(1,500)	(26,000)
Cost of sales		(1,050)	(2,100)	(3,150)	(5,250)	(6,300)	(7,350)	(5,250)	(2,100)	(6,300)	(6,300)	(6,300)	(3,150)	(54,600)
Gross profit (sales less cost of sales)		1,450	2,900	4,350	7,250	8,700	10,150	7,250	2,900	8,700	8,700	8,700	4,350	75,400
Gross margin (gross profit/sales)		58%	58%	58%	58%	58%	58%	58%	58%	58%	58%	58%	58%	58%
Monthly fixed costs														
Sales staff		(1,200)	(1,200)	(1,200)	(1,200)	(1,200)	(1,200)	(1,200)	(1,200)	(1,200)	(1,200)	(1,200)	(1,200)	(14,400)
Admin. staff		(1,500)	(1,500)	(1,500)	(1,500)	(1,500)	(1,500)	(1,500)	(1,500)	(1,500)	(1,500)	(1,500)	(1,500)	(18,000)
Rent		(1,000)	(1,000)	(1,000)	(1,000)	(1,000)	(1,000)	(1,000)	(1,000)	(1,000)	(1,000)	(1,000)	(1,000)	
Promotion		(2,000)	(2,000)	(2,000)	(2,000)	(2,000)	(2,000)	(2,000)	(2,000)	(2,000)	(2,000)	(2,000)	(2,000)	
Total fixed costs		(5,700)	(5,700)	(5,700)	(5,700)	(5,700)	(5,700)	(5,700)	(5,700)	(5,700)	(5,700)	(5,700)	(5,700)	
Profit		(4,250)	(2,800)	(1,350)	1,550	3,000	4,450	1,550	(2,800)	3,000	3,000	3,000	(1,350)	
Profit margin (profit/sales)		(170%)	(56%)	(18%)	12%	20%	25%	12%	(56%)	20%	20%	20%	(18%)	

Best Budget Training Services
Budgeted cash flow (£)

	20X2 Dec	20X3 Jan	Feb	Mar	April	May	June	July	Aug	Sept	Oct	Nov	Dec
Receipts from customers	2,500	5,000	7,500	12,500	15,000	17,500	12,500	5,000	15,000	15,000	15,000	7,500	7,500
Payments													
Delegate materials		(50)	(100)	(150)	(250)	(300)	(350)	(250)	(100)	(300)	(300)	(300)	(150)
Refreshments		(200)	(400)	(600)	(1,000)	(1,200)	(1,400)	(1,000)	(400)	(1,200)	(1,200)	(1,200)	(600)
Venues		(300)	(600)	(900)	(1,500)	(1,800)	(2,100)	(1,500)	(600)	(1,800)	(1,800)	(1,800)	(900)
Trainers' fee		(500)	(1,000)	(1,500)	(2,500)	(3,000)	(3,500)	(2,500)	(1,000)	(3,000)	(3,000)	(3,000)	(1,500)
Sales staff		(1,200)	(1,200)	(1,200)	(1,200)	(1,200)	(1,200)	(1,200)	(1,200)	(1,200)	(1,200)	(1,200)	(1,200)
Admin. staff		(1,500)	(1,500)	(1,500)	(1,500)	(1,500)	(1,500)	(1,500)	(1,500)	(1,500)	(1,500)	(1,500)	(1,500)
Rent		(12,000)	0	0	0	0	0	0	0	0	0	0	0
Promotion		0	(2,000)	(2,000)	(2,000)	(2,000)	(2,000)	(2,000)	(2,000)	(2,000)	(2,000)	(2,000)	(2,000)
Cash flow for month	2,500	(10,750)	700	4,650	5,050	6,500	450	(4,950)	8,200	4,000	4,000	(3,500)	(350)
Opening balance	0	2,500	(8,250)	(7,550)	(2,900)	2,150	8,650	9,100	4,150	12,350	16,350	20,350	16,850
Closing balance	2,500	(8,250)	(7,550)	(2,900)	2,150	8,650	9,100	4,150	12,350	16,350	20,350	16,850	16,500

Best Budget Training Services
Budgeted income statement (£)

	Month: October 20X3			YTD 10 months to October 20X3			Full year		
	Actual	Budget	Variance	Actual	Budget	Variance	Actual	Budget	Variance
Courses	7	6	1	45	43	2	55	52	3
Delegates	50	60	(10)	420	430	(10)	500	520	(20)
Sales	11,000	15,000	(4,000)	100,800	107,500	(6,700)	120,000	130,000	(10,000)
Costs varying per delegate									
Delegate materials	(400)	(300)	(100)	(3,360)	(2,150)	(1,210)	(4,000)	(2,600)	(1,400)
Refreshments	(1,050)	(1,200)	150	(8,820)	(8,600)	(220)	(10,500)	(10,400)	(100)
Costs varying per course									
Venues	(2,450)	(1,800)	(650)	(15,750)	(12,900)	(2,850)	(19,250)	(15,600)	(3,650)
Trainers' fee	(3,430)	(3,000)	(430)	(22,050)	(21,500)	(550)	(26,950)	(26,000)	(950)
Cost of sales	(7,330)	(6,300)	(1,030)	(49,980)	(45,150)	(4,830)	(60,700)	(54,600)	(6,100)
Gross profit (sales less cost of sales)	3,670	8,700	(5,030)	50,820	62,350	(11,530)	59,300	75,400	(16,100)
Gross margin (gross profit/sales)	33%	58%		50%	58%		49%	58%	
Monthly fixed costs									
Sales staff	(1,300)	(1,200)	(100)	(13,000)	(12,000)	(1,000)	(15,600)	(14,400)	(1,200)
Admin. staff	(1,400)	(1,500)	100	(14,000)	(15,000)	1,000	(16,800)	(18,000)	1,200
Rent	(1,000)	(1,000)	0	(10,000)	(10,000)	0	(12,000)	(12,000)	0
Promotion	(2,200)	(2,000)	(200)	(24,000)	(20,000)	(4,000)	(26,400)	(24,000)	(2,400)
Total fixed costs	(5,900)	(5,700)	(200)	(61,000)	(57,000)	(4,000)	(70,800)	(68,400)	(2,400)
Profit	(2,230)	3,000	(5,230)	(10,180)	5,350	(15,530)	(11,500)	7,000	(18,500)
Profit margin (profit/sales)	(20%)	20%		(10%)	5%		(10%)	5%	

Risks, forecasts, balanced scorecards and KPIs

Better budgeting means going a bit further, not just staying within a limit by making savings and delivering more. What measures can we introduce to improve our budgeting approach? How can reforecasts and Key Performance Indicators (KPIs) help us?

The balanced scorecard and strategy maps

We introduced the balanced scorecard in Chapter 1 and many large organisations use one. The balanced scorecard was developed by Professor Robert Kaplan and Dr David Norton in 1992. It includes a number of simple strategic measures with KPIs.

Each KPI may be cascaded down through the organisation and integrated into budgets. Ideally managers will be able to relate their actions and measures back to the overall goals, strategy and objectives of the organisation. The balanced scorecard should translate strategy into performance measurement and delivery.

Kaplan and Norton suggest that the measures are divided into four balanced perspectives, these being:

1 **Financial** – what are the high-level financial measures?
2 **Customers** – how do customers see us?
3 **Internal business processes** – what do we need to excel at?
4 **Learning and innovation** – where can we continue to improve?

Each perspective would normally have around four or five key measures. The balanced scorecard model is not prescriptive – you may choose perspectives that are better for your own business. For example, the largest UK retailer, Tesco, has a 'steering wheel' rather than a balanced scorecard with five perspectives – these being:

1 Financial
2 Customers
3 Operations
4 People
5 Community.

The standard balanced scorecard only has the four balanced perspectives compared to Tesco's five. But however many perspectives a firm lists the financial perspective is still at the top!

The interesting notable addition for Tesco is 'community' and it is easy to see how the UK's biggest and the world's third biggest retailer needs to sell itself to the communities in which it operates. What might be the special extra 'perspective' for your organisation?

You may not have a balanced scorecard within your organisation, although you probably do have some KPIs. Ideally, like the balanced scorecard, some of your KPIs should be ultimately linked to the strategy of your organisation. When you manage your budgets it is not just a case of managing costs, it is also a matter of delivering the KPIs.

Examples of linking KPIs to strategy

- A company may have a strategic plan to retain and win customers through providing superior customer service. It would make sense for the company to design measures around how customer service was perceived by customers relative to competitors. The next stage would be to set a target for this measure to be reached or be improved by.

- The company may aim to gain competitive advantage through being the largest supplier within a given market. Under this criterion it makes sense to have measures based around market share relative to competitors.

Exercise

1 Do you or other managers in your organisation have KPIs that are linked to the organisation's strategy?

2 If they are not, how could they be?

In 2004 Kaplan and Norton developed their ideas further with 'strategy maps'.[1]

The strategy map is a diagram of the organisation's strategic goals laying out what has to be achieved in each perspective in order to achieve the overall objectives of the organisation. These maps normally include links between the goals in different perspectives. For example a map might feature a goal to improve customer service (customer perspective) through improving staff customer service skills (learning and innovation perspective).

Strategy maps were developed after balanced scorecards and are therefore often seen as an add-on or an extra. Despite this, they should actually precede the construction of a balanced scorecard.

KPIs and budgets

Example

A fast food outlet might be able to cut staff costs easily – but by doing this they may then damage the speed of service. Speed might have been the key requirement of customers – so by damaging speed of service, sales will be lost. It would be better to challenge the outlet manager to reduce costs but also deliver a number of KPIs.

Exercise

1 What are the KPIs used within your organisation or department?

2 How do you integrate the delivery of the KPIs within the building and management of your budgets?

3 Can you define the key outputs and outcomes (the results from the outputs) that your department or unit needs to deliver to help the organisation deliver its objectives?

▶

1 Kaplan, R. and Norton, D. (2004) *Strategy Maps: Converting Intangible Assets into Tangible Outcomes*, Harvard Business School Press.

> **4** Can you express these as a simple KPI? If you manage others perhaps you could set some simple KPIs alongside the budget.

Values, mission and vision statements – and budgets

Values, mission and vision statements may seem very remote from the role of the budget manager but should be seen as fundamentally important if they are genuinely followed by the organisation.

Statements of value, mission and vision are loved by major companies wishing to express some grand ideals and ambitions. If these statements are truthful then budgets should be linked back to what actually happens in the organisation. Often though, these statements mean very little and tend not to be known or understood by managers. The statements often include platitudes which could apply to any organisation.

Jack Welch, the former CEO of General Electric, has little time for these kinds of statements. He believes that statements and values should be replaced with statements about behaviours. Organisations should therefore ask themselves 'What behaviour do we want our managers to exhibit?' Demonstrating this behaviour offers rewards, but in the harsh corporate world of America, failing to demonstrate the preferred behaviour can result in a penalty, even dismissal.

A mission statement is a statement of why an organisation exists. A vision statement is a statement about where the company sees itself in the future. These statements often talk of excellence and integrity being key virtues in the organisation. Perhaps what really matters is how these virtues are demonstrated.

Ideally, vision statements should include some relative measures. Here is the vision statement from a Thai oil company, PTT. Each element of its vision statement is expressed in a relative and quantifiable form. This gives the managers within PTT a clear target of what the company aims to achieve and by when. Strategies and budgets should then be formulated with the aim of achieving these long-term quantified objectives.

PTT's vision

PTT will be:

1 **BIG** – a world scale company to be listed in Fortune 100[2] by 2020.

2 **LONG** – a company with sustainable growth to be listed in DJSI[3] in 2013.

3 **STRONG** – operational excellence to achieve top quartile performance (against peers) by 2020.

Source: PTT 2010 annual report and accounts.

These all have clearly quantifiable measures. Each measure includes benchmarking against other firms and so they are therefore relative performance measures. If other firms improve their performance then PTT needs to improve to 'keep up'.

Exercise

Do you think either of these statements could capture the imagination of employees to influence their motivation, decision making and budgeting?

■ Fujifilm – 'Kill Kodak'.

■ Komatsu Limited (construction and mining equipment) – 'Encircle Caterpillar'.

The succinct 'Kill Kodak' may sound a little humorous but also slightly shocking. The statements for both Fujifilm and Komatsu attempt to quantify success other than by beating their main global competitor.

It is probably unacceptable to use such statements in most organisations, but worth considering that the success of your organisation is probably at the expense of your competitors. How can you communicate this message easily to employees? Like the above statements, the fewer the words, the clearer the message.

---

2 Fortune 100 (100 biggest public companies by revenue in the world). PTT plans to increase its revenue to over US $140 billion, so profit might be a better target.
3 DJSI – Dow Jones Sustainability Indexes – track the performance of 'sustainability' driven companies.

Exercise

1 Does your organisation have statements about values, mission and vision? If it does, do you know what the statements are and how these statements relate to how you build and manage your budgets? (Values, mission and vision statements can normally be found at the start of large PLCs' annual reports and accounts.)

2 If organisations want to deliver their vision, they have to communicate it effectively to the employees who are going to deliver it. The values, mission, vision and strategy of the organisation should be integrated into the construction and management of budgets. How could these be better communicated within your own organisation?

Risks and budgets

Risk is the probability of an event occurring multiplied by the cost, or impact of it occurring. The only way to avoid all risk in business is not to be in business at all. Business means risk, but the risks that a company takes should be proportional to the potential returns. Different businesses have different appetites for risk. If a company avoids all risk it will potentially paralyse the business. In many industries change and uncertainty have increased in recent years, thus increasing risk.

To incorporate risks within budgets we need to identify potential events, their probability and their impact. These can then be formally listed in a log and managed.

It is also important to encourage managers to think about risks in their day-to-day budget management. They should be asking themselves, 'What might happen and what would the consequence be?' It is impossible to plan for the unknown and the unexpected; *it is* possible to encourage managers to be responsive to change. The adoption of reforecasting and rolling forecasts (as described in Chapter 2) may encourage managers to identify risks earlier and therefore identify appropriate action.

Potential approaches to the risks are:

■ risk avoidance – eliminating risk
■ risk reduction – reducing the likelihood of the event or mitigating its impact

■ risk sharing or transfer – get other organisations to take on all or part of the risk

■ risk acceptance.

Exercise

Think about your own organisation and department. For each, list out the major risks (the events and their impact), and summarise how these are or could be managed or mitigated.

Examples

■ **Risk** – a customer may go bankrupt.

■ **Solution** – risks may be reduced with credit insurance.

■ **Risk** – a contractor may deliver a project late.

■ **Solution** – the contract may include a penalty for late delivery.

■ **Risk** – investment in plant and machinery is under-recovered due to lower than expected customer orders.

■ **Solution** – contract with customers for minimum order levels before committing to the investment, or get customers to directly fund the investment.

■ **Risk** – an airline takes a risk over the future of fuel prices.

■ **Solution** – contract to buy fuel at a fixed rate for a period into the future. But be careful, this could backfire. In 2008/09 fuel prices dropped resulting in a number of airlines that had 'hedged' the price making large losses: Cathay Pacific lost nearly US $1 billion on fuel price hedging.

Risk can be an opportunity to make more profit. In some instances companies may be able to manage risks better than their customers or suppliers and it may be worthwhile taking on risks and charging customers a premium, and gaining discounts on suppliers.

10

Delegating budgets to others

Delegating budgets can help to give budget responsibility to those who are best placed to control costs. But be careful as without proper training and organisation the results can be disastrous.

What is the best way to delegate and ensure that those with budget responsibility are appropriately trained to do the job to their best ability?

Why delegate?

By delegating budgets, we are delegating authority and responsibility. Ideally authority and responsibility should go to the managers who can make the best decisions. You should not aim to delegate budgets with the idea of getting rid of work and problems!

Some people believe budgets should be left to accountants, but who is it that you want to be making the decisions in your organisation: accountants or managers? For example marketing decisions should be made by marketing managers and engineering decisions should be made by engineers.

Devolved or delegated budgets

In the early 1990s many police forces in England, Wales and Scotland started to delegate budgets to police officers. Previously, budgets were controlled and managed centrally. In order to give more power, authority and responsibility to operational police officers, budgets had to be devolved, or delegated.

In order for the police forces to manage devolved budgets they needed to employ a number of extra accountants and develop financial systems to provide better management information. Without first developing the support infrastructure budgets could not be delegated.

Once police officers had the budgets they could make decisions, but had to make these decisions whilst also considering their financial impact. Before having delegated budgets, overtime may have been authorised without full consideration of the cost. With delegated budgets, managers (or police officers) now had to consider if the cost of the overtime was worth the outcome that it would deliver, and make decisions about how limited resources could be best utilised to deliver the best results.

In order to devolve or delegate these budgets successfully many forces introduced a programme of basic financial training. This training encouraged officers to think about the financial impact of their actions and decisions and also worked to sell the ideas of devolved budgeting.

In the UK, budgets have been devolved in many other public sector organisations such as the National Health Service (NHS) and in schools.

The rationale for devolved or delegated budgets

The theory is that some decisions are best made by junior and middle managers. These junior and middle managers may be doctors, nurses, teachers, lecturers or even accountants. They make their decisions based on their professional judgements and (with the introduction of budgets) consideration of the financial consequences of their decisions.

Without being given budgets it may not be possible to delegate authority for management decisions. There are critics of delegated budgets within public sector organisations such as hospitals and schools. An often stated view is that doctors, nurses and teachers should concentrate on what they do best rather than being involved in petty administration. These critics miss the important point that budgets give power to these professionals to make better choices using their professional background. Budgets are principally about managing and making decisions and taking responsibility for them; they should not be about petty bureaucracy, form filling and spreadsheets.

By delegating budgets, an organisation is delegating authority and responsibility. Ideally management decisions should be made by managers in the best position, with the best knowledge and skills to make those decisions, and a delegated budget recognises this.

Above we described how several of the UK's police forces delegated budgets to police officers. The idea behind the move was that police officers were the best individuals to make decisions about policing. By giving budgets to police officers they were able to make those decisions but also had to carry the financial consequences of those decisions within their budgets. Before the budgets were devolved the officers usually needed training, which included some basic budget principles and systems but also had to sell them the idea that the budget should be their responsibility. Officers were more enthusiastic about the budgets when they could see some direct benefits within their areas.

Delegating budgets may mean the creation of the 'budgeting game' (discussed earlier in this book on p. 99). Under the 'budgeting game' people waste time not on management decisions but on manipulating the budget and its rules. Budget managers may focus on what is best for them and their departments rather than what is best for the organisation as a whole. These criticisms of delegated budgets may be partly countered with careful training and design in the budgeting systems.

McGregor's theory X and theory Y

Your approach to delegating budgets and managing managers with budgets depends upon your view of the managers and how they are motivated. In 1961 Douglas McGregor (MIT Sloan School of Management) introduced the idea of theory X and theory Y approaches to management. These are two different approaches which are based on a manager's view of employees.

Theory X

The managers assume employees are lazy and will avoid work. Employees need to be closely supervised and controlled. Under this view it would be very difficult to delegate budgets at all. If budgets are delegated, they are delegated with strict controls and regulations. Budget managers are not encouraged to make their own decisions and act autonomously.

Theory Y

The managers assume that their employees are self-motivated. They feel they can rely on employees to try to do the right thing. Under this view, one would be happy to delegate control and decision making. Managers would be keen to encourage people to act on their own initiative to make the right decisions for the benefit of the organisation. Any delegation involves trust.

The key to successful delegation

1 Make the budgets that are delegated significant

It is essential to identify the decision makers to whom you are going to delegate budgets and decide what costs you want them to manage. Delegating trivial amounts might lead to petty cost control.

For example, if you just give someone a budget for their stationery they may focus on controlling the issue of paper and pens when the main costs within the organisation may well be staff time. It is important also to educate managers about how they can influence costs. It is very tempting for budget managers to focus on the costs they feel they have the most discretion over rather than on the costs that are the most important.

2 Match authority and responsibility

Make sure there is the best match between authority and responsibility that you can achieve. There is no point in giving managers budgets for costs they cannot control. Do not delegate their budgets and then make decisions about the expenditure for them.

The perfect alignment between budget responsibility and budget authority may not always be easily achieved. The cost performance of one department may be dependent upon the performance of other departments. The delegated budgets might encourage the mentality of 'silo thinking', with departments reluctant to help or interact with other departments unless it helps them achieve their budget.

3 Design tailored training and develop budget management confidence

We train many managers in a lot of different organisations and different countries on budgeting and forecasting. We often find that they are confused by accounting terminology and principles.

Terminology should be kept straightforward and when used explained concisely. Basic finance training is often useful, covering an understanding of accounting principles (particularly accruals accounting and the difference between profit and cash) and the principles of costs and cost management (including proactive approaches to manage and reduce costs).

New budget managers often lack confidence so should be reassured that they have been given the responsibility of managing a budget because they are the experts in that particular part of the organisation's activities.

In many organisations, experienced budget managers are self-taught, often learning 'on the job' or from their managers. This is not always the best approach and may perpetuate bad budget management practice.

A better approach is first to identify the good budget managers, and then identify how they are managing their budgets. These managers should be encouraged to share their knowledge and experience with their peers. If you have the resources and the managers have time, you could also organise formal budget training, which promotes best practice for your organisation. You can tailor the content of the programme with case studies that model the reports and information used by managers. Think about the types of decisions managers make and how these affect their budget.

4 Recognise the increasing need for speed

Generally organisations are getting flatter (fewer levels of management) and faster (with rapidly changing technology and markets). Budgetary control systems should reflect this as managers need to be able to make decisions quickly.

Effective delegation needs quicker reporting and quicker response times. Budget managers need to operate proactively, identifying problems before they arise. A combination of forecasting and 'leading' (as opposed to 'lagging') key performance indicators (KPIs) will help them.

5 Consider internal markets and transfer pricing

In some organisations, in an attempt to improve efficiency and cost effectiveness, internal markets are established. This is where budget holders effectively buy services from internal providers. This internal market is often criticised as it provides extra bureaucracy and sets departments against one another.

It may be that the internal market challenges managers to examine the costs of internal services which would be otherwise free. The service provider has to justify its costs and may also be encouraged to find savings. When goods and services are provided freely it is very difficult to be careful with them and often results in extravagance. An internal charge counters this attitude. Just because an internal market is established it does not necessarily mean that the internal buyers have the option of purchasing goods and services from outside the organisation.

In the UK, the NHS constantly wrestles with internal market structures to try to improve efficiency. While it may be that no market structure can be truly perfect, it may still though, encourage greater efficiency and cost effectiveness. Once an internal market has delivered improvements there is a good case for scrapping it.

Transfer prices are the internal prices between parts of the organisation. For example, between a manufacturing unit in one country and sales unit in another country, or between two factories.

If you operate an internal market or have transfer prices, you should be wary of artificial internal 'profit' figures. The only true profit is profit earned from real outside customers. It is important to try to encourage managers to maximise the profits for the organisation rather than for their business unit.

11

Beyond budgeting

> The process of management is not about administering fixed budgets, it is about the dynamic allocation of resources.
>
> *Lord Browne, ex-CEO, BP*

The 'beyond budgeting' approach advocates an alternative approach to budgets. Can this really work in your organisation?

Introduction

The 'beyond budgeting' approach challenges the role of budgets. It also questions whether or not organisations actually need budgets at all. Can we deliver the objectives of a budget through some other means?

New approaches and ideas in business and management techniques normally originate from one of three sources:

1 academic institutions such as Harvard Business School (the balanced scorecard)

2 management consultancies such as the Boston Consulting Group (the 'Boston Consulting Group growth share matrix')

3 businesses developing their own alternative approaches.

Tools and techniques originating from either academia or consultancies tend to have structured and sometimes prescriptive 'branded' frameworks. Tools and techniques developed within businesses tend to evolve over time and often present a more varied range of approaches.

The beyond budgeting approach originates from business and, because of this, lacks a standard framework. Different businesses, with their own different approaches, have different solutions. There are some umbrella organisations, that seek to develop and share good practice. The Beyond Budgeting Roundtable is the leading group (see **www.bbrt.org**) and it has started to produce beyond budgeting framework models based on the combined experiences of a number of organisations.

There are a number of major organisations that are interested in applying beyond budgeting principles. Many of the case studies and examples are from Scandinavian companies, the most notable of which are:

- Handelsbanken, a Swedish bank
- Borealis, a Scandinavian chemical company (now headquarted in Austria)
- StatoilHydro, a Norwegian oil company.

Other companies said to be interested in 'beyond budgeting' include Google, Unilever, Southwest Airlines, Toyota, Telekom Malaysia and Leyland Trucks.[1]

Are budgets bad for business?

Some of the main criticisms of traditional budgets have already been discussed in this book. Some of the specific criticisms of budgets from the beyond budgeting movement are that they:

- are too resource and time consuming
- are slow to detect problems
- are unreliable for performance evaluation
- quickly date
- are a source of 'game playing' and office politics (e.g. effort may be wasted on getting more resources from other parts of the organisation rather than beating the competition)
- require financial targets that often overwhelm what is good for the business and ultimately the business owners
- over-emphasise short-term financial measures

1 Numerous cases are documented in Hope, J. and Fraser, R. (2003) *Beyond Budgeting: How Managers Can Break Free from the Annual Performance Trap*, Harvard Business School Press.

- are often departmental based which may encourage 'silo thinking' (this is when departments focus on what is best for them and remain divorced from the rest of the business, with each department operating as it is in its own silo)
- are disruptive to cooperation
- are disruptive to innovation and adaption to changing conditions and opportunities
- lack in rigour.

The beyond budgeting solution to these problems is to completely do away with budgets. There is a lot of appeal to this approach, but most readers of this book will not have the opportunity to make such a change so a more realistic approach is to review each of the criticisms of traditional budgets and try to find a solution to enable them to work better. Perhaps some of the ideas of beyond budgeting can be adapted and incorporated within your traditional budgeting system?

Beyond budgeting does not mean necessarily switching completely to rolling forecasts (see Chapter 2), but rolling forecasts do normally feature prominently in most beyond budgeting approaches.

Probably the main deficiency with budgets arises from the performance measurement aspect. Earlier in this book we quoted Jack Welch from GE. His view is 'Don't beat the budget beat the competition'. Beyond budgeting often advocates alternative performance measurement approaches often featuring something similar to a balanced scorecard.

When designing performance measurement systems managers should not be too reliant on beating internally generated targets. It would be better to set performance measurement as a relative target – then see how well you are doing at matching or beating peer group organisations. There should also be non-financial targets focusing on key elements to deliver the organisation's strategy and customer satisfaction (or delight!).

Beyond budgeting requires a management culture of trust, where we trust our managers and teams to 'do the right thing' for the business and the shareholders. This probably requires us to adopt a theory Y approach to management (see Chapter 10). One might think that these ideas are only for certain businesses in certain business cultures, countries (Scandinavia is the birthplace and 'home' of beyond budgeting) and industries. However, the approach is being explored in a wide range of different businesses and locations.

Many companies are working out their own ideas and solutions rather than relying on consultants and as a result of this there is no standard uniform model of how to manage a business effectively without budgets. The beyond budgeting approach continues to develop and 12 basic principles have been developed by the Beyond Budgeting Roundtable (see **www.bbrt.org**).

These principles are organised into the following four groups:

1 Governance and transparency
2 Accountable teams
3 Goals and rewards
4 Planning and controls.

The principles and groups are listed in full in Table 11.1.

In summary, going 'beyond budgets' or scrapping budgets completely requires major changes in culture, systems, performance measurement and the basis of rewards.

Exercise

Reading through the list opposite you can probably see a theme of trust and of self-management. Central to the beyond budgeting approach is the adoption of a 'theory Y' style of management.

1 Does your organisation trust you to just 'do the right thing' or do they need to micromanage you with controls?

2 Do you trust people who report to you to 'do the right thing' or do you impose some controls? The beyond budgeting approach suggests that the 'command and control' budgeting system is all about asserting central control, yet many organisations have created and devolved budgets precisely because they want to delegate authority, responsibility and control.

Implementing beyond budgeting

Many of the main advocates of beyond budgeting stress the importance of completely scrapping the budget; you might believe that they would wish the word budget to be banned! A compelling case for beyond budgeting is made by Bjarte Bogsnes in his book

table 11.1	The 12 beyond budgeting principles

Governance and transparency

1. Values	Bind people to a common cause; *not a central plan*
2. Governance	Govern through shared values and sound judgement; *not detailed rules and regulations*
3. Transparency	Make information open and transparent; *don't restrict and control it*

Accountable teams

4. Teams	Organise around a seamless network of accountable teams; *not centralised functions*
5. Trust	Trust teams to regulate their performance; *don't micro-manage them*
6. Accountability	Base accountability on holistic criteria and peer reviews; *not on hierarchical relationships*

Goals and rewards

7. Goals	Set ambitious medium-term goals; *not short-term fixed targets*
8. Rewards	Base rewards on relative performance; *not on fixed targets*

Planning and controls

9. Planning	Make planning a continuous and inclusive process; *not a top-down annual event*
10. Co-ordination	Co-ordinate interactions dynamically; *not through annual budgets*
11. Resources	Make resources available just-in-time; *not just-in-case*
12. Controls	Base controls on fast, frequent feedback; *not budget variances*

Source: The Beyond Budgeting Roundtable, 2011, **www.bbrt.org**.

Implementing Beyond Budgeting.[2] One thing that makes his book so appealing is that he does not sell beyond budgeting as an approach

---

2 Bogsnes, B. (2008) *Implementing Beyond Budgeting: Unlocking the Performance Potential*, John Wiley. This book also contains recent cases of beyond budgeting.

without any problems and challenges. In fact he suggests that the beyond budgeting approach requires a process of evolution to develop better systems and processes to deliver the best performance. Within his book he reviews three case studies: Handelsbanken, Borealis and StatoilHydro. Bogsnes writes with some authority as he is the only person to have been involved in two major implementations of the beyond budgeting approach (Borealis and StatoilHydro).

For StatoilHydro, Bogsnes outlines five principles that underpin its approach to beyond budgeting.

1 Performance should be about beating similar companies' performance, not a fixed budget. You might remember the excellent quote from Jack Welch about beating the competition and not the budget. Performance measurement should be based on some relative measure of performance against comparable businesses.

2 Managers should be encouraged to do the 'right thing'. They are guided as to what is the right thing by the following:
  – The StatoilHydro book – this book lays out the values, principles and policies of StatoilHydro.
  – 'Ambition to Action' – this is StatoilHydro's equivalent of the balanced scorecard: it translates strategy and 'ambition' into actions and measures.
  – Decision criteria – the rules under which decisions are justified and made.
  – Authorities – even without budgets managers have limited authority.
  – Sound business judgement – this suggests a business 'common sense' check on decisions and actions.

There is of course a cultural aspect of doing the 'right thing'. No doubt some of the managers in Lehman Brothers, WorldCom and Enron all believed they were doing the 'right thing' for their businesses and making sound business decisions. What is deemed appropriate attitude and behaviour changes over time. Managers need to be educated in what complies with the ethics of their business. StatoilHydro presents its view of what is 'right' in the StatoilHydro book. Think about the different businesses you have worked with or know. Do they have different ideas of what behaviour is 'right'? Grand statements of standards and ethics are not necessarily reality. Enron's motto 'Respect, Integrity, Communication and Excellence' did not quite match its true culture.

3 Resources are not allocated by a budget but on a case-by-case basis. This requires an ongoing review process or a well-designed set of decision criteria (i.e. what a business case needs to demonstrate to win approval).

4 When reviewing performance, managers should look to the future and what actions they are going to take rather than dwelling on the past. This is a principle which we advocate when managing conventional budgets. Under the beyond budgeting regime, budgets are scrapped and forecasts developed. If you are still, like most companies, using the conventional approach to budgets you can supplement this with the use of forecasts to encourage managers to be more forward thinking and proactive in their management of resources.

5 Performance evaluation assesses what has been delivered and how managers have behaved. Under Jack Welch's regime at GE managers were rewarded for delivering and harshly punished for failing. Within StatoilHydro the evaluation of managers' performance is only partly dependent on what they deliver; they are also rewarded for how they behave. Jack Welch is very critical of statements about 'values' which are often full of platitudes. Despite being heavily focused around delivering the traditional 'bottom line' performance he also believes it is important not to talk about values but to talk about 'behaviours'.

Bogsnes stresses that the success or failure of beyond budgeting is more likely to be down to its implementation rather than its design. Within StatoilHydro he describes how different individuals embraced the beyond budgeting principles at different rates with different levels of enthusiasm. It is probably inevitable that some managers will find it difficult to move from the world of budgets that they have been used to for all their working lives. The transition should include education and support for managers to help them change attitudes and behaviour.

Achieving objectives obliquely – obliquity

Do the most tightly controlled, planned and profit focused businesses perform best? Not according to John Kay (**www.johnkay.com**), weekly columnist at the *Financial Times* and renowned author and economist. In his 2010 book *Obliquity* he suggests that often the best results are achieved by working 'obliquely'. Is Google a fantastic business success because it is so focused on profit or because it is so focused on giving users the best search results and experience?

Did the failed bank Lehman Brothers deliver the best results to share-holders by heavily incentivising employees to focus on profit? John Kay extends this idea beyond business – perhaps the rich people are not the ones most focused on being rich, the happiest might not be the ones most focused on pursuing happiness, the most successful cities are not the most planned.

To be a success in any business you first need to deliver value to customers. There is a danger with budgets that are just focused on profit and costs that this gets lost. We need to make our staff enthusiastic about delivering a good job and being the best we can. Perhaps better performance normally comes more from motivation and attitude rather than better measurement and targets. We should design our budgeting approach to be flexible enough to allow managers to 'do the right thing' when they have to. This is part of the thinking behind beyond budgeting.

Conclusion

There are some interesting ideas being developed on the future of budgets and measuring and managing performance within organi-sations but most readers of this book will not be able to rip up the budget and start a completely new and radical approach. We need to understand why it is not working properly and try to identify some changes to make it better. I have some sympathy with the beyond budgeting view that budgets will always be flawed, but some of the flaws may be minimised. The important question is not whether budgets are perfect but whether overall they help the organisation deliver its objectives. In addition, how can we try to make them function better?

Beyond budgeting, John Kay's obliquity and Kaplan and Norton's balanced scorecard all suggest we need to think about performance in terms other than just profit or cost performance today. Can you influence your organisation to make some moves towards this thinking? What are the main things your organisation needs to do to ensure it wins at what it does? Can we measure our progress towards this and develop some measures that encourage our managers to deliver?

Reviewing your budgeting and forecasting performance

12

What lessons have you learned?

Having built and managed a budget, what have you learned from the experience? How can you improve things? And what comes next?

Take action and responsibility

To get the most out of this book for yourself and your organisation you need to:

- Take some personal responsibility for making improvements in budgeting and forecasting in your organisation.
- Take responsibility for your own development.
- Take some positive action.
- Encourage your colleagues to follow your lead.

Throughout the book you will have attempted a number of self-coaching question and answer exercises. These exercises are designed to challenge you to think about the ideas within this book and how they can be practically applied in your day-to-day work in your organisation. Many of the book's exercises can also be used for team discussions and development.

Personal action plans

We recommend you review each of the exercises and try to construct your own personal action plan. This action plan will include not only what you are going to do to improve budgets and forecasts within your organisation but also what you going to do to take your development forward.

Unfortunately many personal action plans tend to be slightly fanciful and do not result in much action. Make yours realistic by avoiding including too many actions. It is much better to have an action plan with five things that you are actually going to do this month rather than have 35 things that you might like to do over the next year.

To make it more likely that you will follow through with this action plan, for each item you identify include a target completion date. By writing this date you will increase your commitment and the chances of you actually completing the plan! If you share your action plan with someone else the chances of you delivering your plan will also be increased.

You will also need to review your progress – perhaps at the end of each month.

To structure your action plans and help you review the book we suggest you make a list of headings following the book's 11 chapters. Under each heading list some actions you are going to take and when. (We have included a template based upon the chapter headings for you to fill in below.) You then need to list out the actions in date order, perhaps writing them in a diary. Cross the actions off as you complete them and you will then be able to gauge your progress.

In each chapter there are questions, some of these are to prompt you for an action you could take. Remember to prune your list of actions to a realistic number.

Templates to review your learning and construct an action plan

Review your progress by ticking off your actions as you complete them and jot down any problems you are encountering. Try to think about how these can be overcome. You will also need to record your personal success or failure at effective budgeting and forecasting, and not just think of this process as a personal development log.

Chapter 1: What is the budget for?

My key learning from this chapter

1.
2.
3.

My actions – with a date when they will be completed

1.
2.
3.

List budgeting and forecasting successes and failures (or learning lessons) related to this heading. Keep updating the list to show progress in your budgeting and forecasting skills.

Chapter 2: What is a forecast and how does it differ from a budget?

My key learning from this chapter

1.
2.
3.

My actions – with a date when they will be completed

1.
2.
3.

List budgeting and forecasting successes and failures (or learning lessons) related to this heading. Keep updating the list to show progress in your budgeting and forecasting skills.

Chapter 3: Essential background financial skills for budgeting

My key learning from this chapter

1.

2.

3.

My actions – with a date when they will be completed

1.

2.

3.

List budgeting and forecasting successes and failures (or learning lessons) related to this heading. Keep updating the list to show progress in your budgeting and forecasting skills.

Chapter 4: How should the budget be built?

My key learning from this chapter

1.

2.

3.

My actions – with a date when they will be completed

1.

2.

3.

List budgeting and forecasting successes and failures (or learning lessons) related to this heading. Keep updating the list to show progress in your budgeting and forecasting skills.

Chapter 5: How should cash be budgeted and controlled?

My key learning from this chapter

1.
2.
3.

My actions – with a date when they will be completed

1.
2.
3.

List budgeting and forecasting successes and failures (or learning lessons) related to this heading. Keep updating the list to show progress in your budgeting and forecasting skills.

Chapter 6: How should capital expenditure be budgeted for?

My key learning from this chapter

1.
2.
3.

My actions – with a date when they will be completed

1.
2.
3.

List budgeting and forecasting successes and failures (or learning lessons) related to this heading. Keep updating the list to show progress in your budgeting and forecasting skills.

Chapter 7: Back to basics – living within your means and delivering VFM

My key learning from this chapter

1.

2.

3.

My actions – with a date when they will be completed

1.

2.

3.

List budgeting and forecasting successes and failures (or learning lessons) related to this heading. Keep updating the list to show progress in your budgeting and forecasting skills.

Chapter 8: Making sense of standard costing and variances

My key learning from this chapter

1.

2.

3.

My actions – with a date when they will be completed

1.

2.

3.

List budgeting and forecasting successes and failures (or learning lessons) related to this heading. Keep updating the list to show progress in your budgeting and forecasting skills.

Chapter 9: Risks, forecasts, balanced scorecards and KPIs

My key learning from this chapter

1.
2.
3.

My actions – with a date when they will be completed

1.
2.
3.

List budgeting and forecasting successes and failures (or learning lessons) related to this heading. Keep updating the list to show progress in your budgeting and forecasting skills.

Chapter 10: Delegating budgets to others

My key learning from this chapter

1.
2.
3.

My actions – with a date when they will be completed

1.
2.
3.

List budgeting and forecasting successes and failures (or learning lessons) related to this heading. Keep updating the list to show progress in your budgeting and forecasting skills.

Chapter 11: Beyond budgeting

My key learning from this chapter

1.

2.

3.

My actions – with a date when they will be completed

1.

2.

3.

List budgeting and forecasting successes and failures (or learning lessons) related to this heading. Keep updating the list to show progress in your budgeting and forecasting skills.

Beyond action plans: how do you know you have been successful?

You have studied this book, applied your action plan and tried some of the ideas, tools and techniques, but has it delivered for you? Some measurement is easy, for example it is possible to measure the accuracy of our forecasts and aim for improvement (see Chapter 2), but accuracy is not the same as usefulness or effectiveness.

Your budgeting and forecasting will be deemed to be better if it delivers a better result for you and your organisation. Some of the improvements will be easier to measure, for example current cash flow and profitability, others such as longer-term improvements, likely profitability and cash flow will be more subjective.

If you have a manager, perhaps one measure is how they view your budgeting and forecasting skills. In most large organisations there will be a formal annual appraisal process. Unfortunately this is often not taken as seriously as it should be. If you have an appraisal, take the opportunity to discuss with your manager your budgeting and forecasting skills, how these have improved and how they might be further improved. If you feel confident of your improvement you want your manager to recognise it; if you are not you may benefit from their feedback or advice. You may feel your manager's own skills may need some development – you could tactfully give them this book. If you have been given this book by a subordinate it is because they value its content, rather than they doubt your abilities!

If you are running your own business then your budgeting success should be reflected in your business's performance. Take some time to review your budgeting and forecasting and how you feel it has improved. Could it improve further?

Index

FINANCIAL TIMES
Essential Guides

9780273761136

9780273757986

9780273757993

9780273768135

9780273772217

9780273772422

Available to buy online and from all good bookshops
www.pearson-books.com